In Quest of the Unicorn Bird

In Quest
of the
Unicorn Bird

*

Oliver Greenfield

MICHAEL JOSEPH
LONDON

MICHAEL JOSEPH LTD

Published by the Penguin Group
27 Wrights Lane, London W8 5TZ, England
Viking Penguin Inc., 375 Hudson Street, New York, New York 10014, USA
Penguin Books Australia Ltd, Ringwood, Victoria, Australia
Penguin Books Canada Ltd, 10 Alcorn Avenue, Suite 300, Toronto, Ontario,
Canada M4V 3B2
Penguin Books (NZ) Ltd, 182–190 Wairau Road, Auckland 10, New Zealand

Penguin Books Ltd, Registered Offices: Harmondsworth, Middlesex, England

First published in Great Britain 1992

Typeset in 11/13pt Imprint
Printed and bound in Great Britain by
Butler & Tanner Ltd, Frome and London

A CIP catalogue record for this book is available from the British Library
ISBN 0 7181 3561 X

The moral right of the author has been asserted

For my mother, father
and Liz

Contents

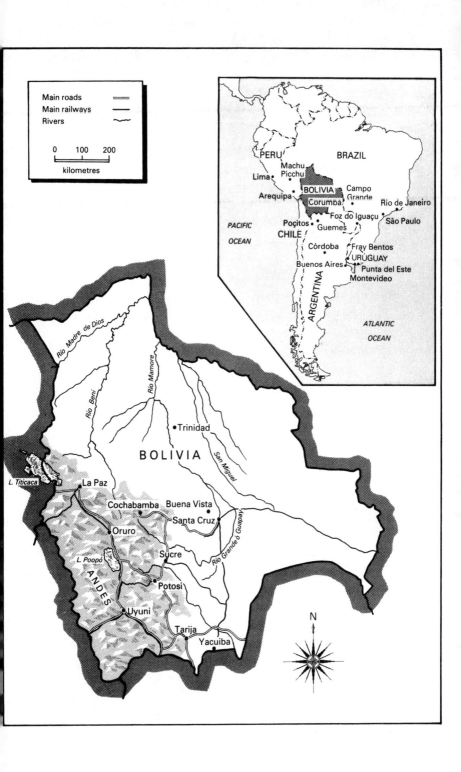

Main roads
Main railways
Rivers

0   100   200
kilometres

PERU   BRAZIL
        Machu
Lima   Picchu
        BOLIVIA   Campo
Arequipa   Corumba   Grande
                        Rio de Janeiro
            Foz do Iguaçu
Poçitos   São Paulo
CHILE   Guemes

PACIFIC
OCEAN

        Córdoba   Fray Bentos
                    URUGUAY
Buenos Aires   Punta del Este
                Montevideo

ARGENTINA

ATLANTIC
OCEAN

Rio Madre de Dios

Rio Beni

Rio Mamore

•Trinidad

BOLIVIA

San Miguel

L. Titicaca

La Paz

Cochabamba   Buena Vista
        Santa Cruz

Oruro

Rio Grande ó Guapay

L. Poopó

Sucre

ANDES

Potosí

Uyuni

Tarija

Yacuiba

N

Chapter 1

*

Proboscis

'Ummmmmm' – a deep resonant booming echoed through the trees.

'Bloody unicorn!' I whispered venomously.

I was sitting in the jungle, the south-westernmost tip of the Amazon, which is in Bolivia. The forest surrounded me with its apparently endless supply of trees, thorns and everything organic that can generate extreme physical discomfort.

It was seven in the morning and I was alone on a rock in my bird hide. The hide was a rectangular frame of branches lashed together with palm rope and palm leaves draped over the frame to complete the camouflage. The sun had been up for two hours, although under the jungle canopy the light range went only from black to not quite so black. Within feet of my hide, a couple of Toco Toucans were busily tucking into a patrol of army ants. Occasionally the wind was strong enough to break the leaf barrier, allowing shafts of sunlight to sneak through, and these rays played on the Toucans' black feathers, creating an iridescent sheen. The illuminated Toucans scooped up the insect soldiers by the battalion, throwing back their heads to funnel the ants down red and yellow banana beaks towards gulping throats. Their elegant white bibs and blue eyeliner made them incongruously comical in their wooded surroundings. They looked slightly over-dressed for a jungle breakfast.

Although I was trying to persuade the Toucans that I was just an oddly shaped extension of the rock I was sitting on and had therefore not moved for over half an hour, the rock's uneven surface was creating an entire sewing-shop of pins and needles in my left buttock. The mosquitos had been up for almost as long as I had and were homing in with a bloodthirsty rage. As I did not wish to scare the Toucans, the mosquito attacks went unchallenged and they obviously concluded that they had stumbled across a free blood bank. The news spread and soon there was a constant blur of wings as they remorselessly bloated themselves on an orgy of my precious blood.

I knew I would soon crack under this barrage of dive-bombing blood suckers but I waited with patient menace until a large mosquito had landed on my hand. I focused my resolve as I watched it prick me with its greedy straw. Still I waited. Its transparent body started to colour red as it swelled with blood. While feeding the mosquito is at its most vulnerable. It has to stop the flow of blood before it can pull out its proboscis and it was therefore momentarily anchored to me. My other hand moved in trained silence. The mosquito was trapped in a dilemma: feed or attempt escape.

Before a decision could be reached, I cupped my hand nonchalantly around it. Holding my prize gently between my fingers I contemplated its death. As my body steadily became more and more poxed with insect bites, I knew I was fighting a losing battle but it was vitally important to my morale that in rare moments like this I should have my revenge. I had pulled off wings, legs and heads in any number of combinations. But the variations were not infinite and so I had to think for a long time before arriving at the ultimate cruelty.

With my nails I nipped off the end of the mosquito's proboscis and released it otherwise unharmed back into the world. It buzzed off, grateful for its reprieve, oblivious to the fact that it would never again be able to feed and would die a lingering death of starvation. My momentary twinge of guilt was curtailed abruptly when another mosquito landed on the corner of my eye and stuck its needle-sharp straw into my eyeball.

The Toucans squawked even more loudly than I did and flapped off, telling all jungle creatures my exact position. Unchallenged by the Toucans, the army ants made quick procession to my hide and invaded. With disproportionately large jaws chomping through everything in their way, they streamed in around me in a wave of black and red. Considering myself no match for a few million of these fanatical warriors, I abandoned the hide and made good my retreat to a conveniently fallen tree trunk. I had been sitting down all of five seconds when the heavens opened with such precocious power it would have caught Noah still varnishing his Ark and before I could shudder I was completely drenched. I was cold, wet, hungry, dirty, and infested with parasites. Sitting numbly on the tree trunk, I silently cursed everything Bolivian and wished tortuous deaths on anyone who had even uttered the word 'Bolivia'. It was then I asked myself with surprising calmness: 'By jove! What the bally heck am I doing here?' – or words to that effect.

CHAPTER 2

*

Building Society

In late June 1988 my father announced he was off to Bolivia, to do some statistical analysis for the government department called the Overseas Development Agency (ODA). This department operates in third world countries advising on many issues but mainly crop and meat production. In Bolivia they had gathered years of data on various crops and production techniques but were unsure of the correct methods of analysis. They had therefore approached my father for his statistical expertise.

Unable to find Bolivia on my wall-map of Europe I checked the 'B's in a the world atlas index. I found out that it is a land-locked country about the size of France and Spain together, right in the centre of the continent of South America.

I was extremely envious of my father and told him of my complete dissatisfaction with my nine-to-five existence. As soon as I had saved some money I was going to pack it all in and go and see the world. I suggested that while he was in South America he should look for a job for me, to which he replied, 'What qualifications shall I offer?' This proved to be a rather difficult question as I had not quite succeeded in traditional educational subjects. I therefore ummed and erred for a minute before replying brightly, 'Enthusiasm.' After discussion we agreed that this was perhaps not quite enough and so with considerable deliberation we decided on 'Enthusiasm and Bigness.'

A month later he returned and I asked him how he had got on. He replied, 'There is a man out there who runs a national park, and he says you can go and work for him.'

Dumbstruck, I had visions of driving Land Rovers down secret jungle paths, wading great rivers, battling with snakes and jaguars. These images flittered around a firm vision of myself dressed in khaki jungle suit complete with pith helmet and rifle, with PARK GUARD embossed in large letters across my chest.

Like many young children, I had been fascinated by animals. But due to hay fever and violent allergies against fur I'd never been able to satiate this interest with standard pets. Instead I had cost my family a fortune as I built up a collection of animal books to rival the Natural History Museum. I then became obsessed with reptiles and amphibians as they had no fur and didn't need hay. From the age of nine I set about with single-minded determination to become the greatest herpetologist in the world.

I consumed reptile books fastidiously, learning the names, size, shape, colour and even habits of all things that crawl or slither. By my eleventh birthday I was a considerable expert and my knowledge was such that I could recite the Latin name of every species of European newt. By then I'd stocked my bedroom and many other parts of the house with every toad, frog, newt and lizard I could catch or my pocket-money could buy. My parents had never discouraged me in these interests, although my mother had drawn the line with snakes. I had considered this extremely inconsiderate at the time but I didn't argue as the crickets I kept to feed my menagerie had recently escaped and it was only a matter of time before my mother asked what was chirping under the floorboards behind the radiator. Also I couldn't count on my sister for support in the snake crusade as she had not yet recovered from finding 'Warty the red-spotted newt' in her wellington boot.

Clearly these thoughts had been in my father's mind when he told the boss of the park that I was an almost internationally renowned amateur herpetologist.

Clarke, the scientific director of the park, was with the aid of two English graduate volunteers all the flora and fauna of an expanse of jungle the size of Wales. They were also studying a species of wild turkey. This and a telephone number to be rung on only one morning a week was the only information my father was able to supply. The discussion between my father and the park director had only lasted a couple of hours and several beers.

I started to appreciate the vagueness of this unpaid job offer and decided it would need a little more consideration before packing in my job to set off for the other side of the world. I resolved to ring the phone number.

Three days later during my lunch hour I left my work place, the Building Society, to ring Bolivia. Equipped with only a ten-pound phone card and the pre-practised phrase 'No hablo Español!' I dialled the fifteen or so digits.

Fortunately I spoke to one of the English graduates, called Valerie. Through the crackle she confirmed that they were all perfectly serious about me joining them in their work. It would be a great help if I would go out as soon as possible. She also asked me if I minded eating vegetarian food as they were all vegetarians. Faced with the most monumental decision in my life so far I found it rather disturbing to be discussing the benefits of vege-tarianism with a voice ten thousand miles away. I con-cluded that she must be mad and so I told her I was particularly fond of carrots. We said our goodbyes and agreed I would let them know when I'd made a decision.

With my head spinning, I slunk back to the Building Society like a circus tiger returning to his cage. I sat at my hierarchically positioned desk, which was piled high with bafflingly boring mortgage files.

I was still staring blankly at a sheet of figures, idly doodling two zeros into a female frontal, when in waltzed the area manager on one of his surprise visits. I quickly shuffled my papers together but he disappeared without a

word into the back office. The branch manager appeared
ten minutes later and my presence was requested. Noticing
my personal development file open on the desk, I sat down
a little apprehensively.

For the next twenty minutes I was cross-examined
about my achievements and thoughts about the job. I
decided to go down fighting and so I lied that although I
liked the work I couldn't afford to stay on at my present
rate of pay. Simply out of necessity I would have to
look for other employment. They nodded, grateful for my
directness and honesty. Then came the pause as the area
manager composed himself for a speech.

'The work you have done has not gone unnoticed. I will
see to an increase in your salary but if you are prepared to
commit yourself to five years of Building Society Institute
Exams I will get you a trainee management position.'

In the slow motion world of building societies, and at
the age of twenty with only ten months' work experience,
I should have considered this great praise. No, I sat horrified at the consequences of accepting this offer. The large
iron gates of responsibility and respectability were forcing
me through, closing behind me, condemning me to a
lifetime of dark sombre suits, loans, mortgages, filing and,
inevitably, a wife.

'A wife!' I saw it all so hideously clearly that I broke
out in a cold sweat and I shuddered trying to shake off
these horrendous thoughts. My only escape was Bolivia.
I forced open my mouth and replied, 'I greatly appreciate
your obvious concern and interest in my future. I therefore
feel I owe you my complete honesty. I've been offered a
post in Bolivia, South America, and I've decided to take
it.'

Their mouths dropped and not a sound was to be heard.
I tried to rally myself to this decision with which my
mouth was happy but my brain was not yet familiar.

Fortunately I recovered first from my little outburst
and I decided that I should offer some sort of explanation.

I therefore added, 'The work is not particularly related to building societies.'

They identified the words 'building societies' with reality and this brought them out of their stupor. They recovered remarkably quickly and said they understood that I should want to go off to do my own thing. The area manager shook me by the hand, wished me luck and told me there might be a job when I got back. My manager took me to the pub and I explained as much as I knew, with a few embellishments to prove the sanity of my decision. We returned to the Building Society and he announced to my curious colleagues, 'Oliver is going to be a Herpetologist in the Amazon Jungle.'

It was only then that the absurdity of the situation struck home but it was too late to change my mind. It had been announced to the world and I was committed. I officially gave in my notice and served the rest of my time. I bought a rucksack, a mosquito net and a single ticket to Rio de Janeiro.

*

CHAPTER 3

One-Way Ticket

I said goodbye to my parents at Heathrow and caught a plane to Paris, Charles de Gaulle Airport. I was still feeling fresh and full of confidence as it had been barely a month since the first phone call.

Having followed the crowds and arrows until I found my jumbo to Rio, I was greeted at the cabin doors by two very attractive French stewardesses. I grasped this brief opportunity to practise the French I had so studiously avoided at school for seven years.

'Bonjour, Madame,' flowed out with bilingual expertise.

They smiled vacantly back. My French exhausted, fortunately the conversation ended as there were a few hundred people waiting behind me to get on. I was very excited when the stewardesses directed me towards the spiral staircase leading to the top floor. I found my seat and settled down to a fourteen-hour flight. Two Germans sitting beside me proceeded to snog and snore alternately for the entire trip. Added to this was the continuous crying of a baby situated behind my left ear. Unable to sleep, I watched the in-flight movie. I had just become accustomed to the wails of the baby and the slurps and grunts of my German neighbours and started to drift off to sleep when clunk, on came the lights and a breakfast tray placed for my inspection.

It was still dark when we arrived at Rio Airport at the foreign time of half-past four in the morning. It was just like any other airport. As I stood staring out of the doors towards the distant lights of the city, I was filled with foreboding. I imagined the flickering lights whispering menacingly, 'This is South America, face it or be swallowed whole!' My confidence wavered and with a shiver I turned away and went to collect my rucksack.

At six the information desk opened and I asked in my best Portuguese, 'When next flight to Santa Cruz, Bolivia?'

'No fly today.'

'Ah.'

The counter woman decided that I'd had my question and that I should move aside for the next person. I stood my ground.

'Ah!' I repeated a little more forcefully.

She sighed and, completely out of character for an information desk, she gave me some information, 'Fly to Santa Cruz from São Paulo today.'

I was carrying all my savings, about three thousand US dollars, hidden around my body and so I was eager to unload before I started to explore. I decided to fly from São Paulo today.

'Okey dokey, where do I get one of those tickets?'

She pointed vaguely in the direction of west. I eventually found the appropriate ticket counter and was told that I couldn't pay in dollars. I went in search of a bank to change my dollars to the local currency, cruzados.

I struggled along the empty corridors dragging my luggage, hoping for a sign of a bank. A little man popped out from behind a pillar. He was a greasy, shifty-looking weasel and he beckoned me saying 'Change'. I was sure the bank wouldn't open for about three hours and I was conscious of the lack of time before the departure of my São Paulo plane. I replied positively, '*Sim*'.

He led me round the corner into a lift and we went between floors to do business. My tour book had advised me that the black market exchange rate was usually better than the official one. However, as the lift doors shut I felt uneasy. In the month before my departure I had conjured up terrible images of the dangers of South America. I was determined not to be caught out at this early stage and satisfied myself that no one was going to jump on me through a hole in the roof.

The little man watched curiously as I tried to look dangerous and asked politely how much I wanted to change. He showed me his exchange rate on his calculator and I scratched my chin pretending to consider. I knew that I was well out of my depth. The figure had at least seven digits. I nodded my consent after a shrewd deliberation.

He couldn't change all I needed but he produced a great wad of notes, which took him about five minutes to count out on a little stool. I had absolutely no idea of the value of the notes, as they were all different sizes, colours and had at leat six zeros. To hide my ignorance I pretended to count with my fingers and said 'Uno, dos, trés' every few seconds. Finally he shuffled all the notes together and held them out in exchange for my dollars. I really started to get the horrors as I imagined this mountain of bills to be only worth about ten pounds. I decided to put his nerve to the test. I took the notes and indicated that I was not happy with his addition. No way could he have my precious dollars until I had counted the cash. He agreed and I knelt at the stool and gave the great stack my best Building Society attention. My fingers blurred nimbly through the notes. I looked up mid count to see him very impressed at my dexterity. Without letting my fingers falter once, I gave him an expert 'I've done this before' smile. Unknown to him, not a single figure was registering in my brain.

I smiled again while trying to give him two bills instead of three, but he was not going to fall for that old one and we laughed together. After leaving the lift he shook my hand firmly in an attempt to convince me of the shrewd deal we had just made but as I had no idea as to the value of the large bulges in my trouser pockets I decided not to repeat the performance.

I went off in search of the bank. True to form it didn't open for a couple of hours but I sat down to wait. A couple of other black market characters offered to change dollars. I searched my repertoire for the 'I wasn't born yesterday' smile. This seemed to cross the language barrier as they walked away grumpily. Meanwhile a large policeman had been eyeing me suspiciously.

I had heard rumours about South American policemen: that they mug you, plant drugs on you or rape you. After twenty hours without sleep and carrying three thousand dollars stuck down my boxer shorts I was prepared to believe anything. So the third time he strode past me I got up and walked off. I looked cautiously behind me to check I'd given him the slip. Sighing my relief I almost bumped into him as he appeared miraculously from behind a pillar. He was about eighteen stones of unpredictable authority with a very large gun slung under his huge gut. To complete the overweight Dirty Harry picture, he wore gold-framed reflector sunglasses.

'Can I 'elp you?'

It occurred to me that he could do whatever he wanted. I slipped back into my Portuguese accent.

'I wait for bank to change money.'

'Bank not open for long time, Section C 'elp you. Follow.'

When a large heavily-armed policeman says 'Follow' I am generally inclined to follow. Endless empty corridors later I was starting to feel a little nervous so I decided to escape. I tried to slip behind large pot plants and pillars. But his jailer instincts told him he was losing me and he would turn giving me a gold-filled encouraging smile and beckon me on.

Realizing I was not going to escape I tried to humour him by making inane comments about the weather. Inane because it was still pitch black. He just grunted. After what seemed an eternity we arrived at Section C, which turned out, rather ominously, to be a hotel.

'It's rape then,' I thought, involuntarily clenching my buttocks.

He marched me to the reception desk clearly intent on booking a double room. He pushed me forward and I whispered hopefully, 'Change'.

The manager nodded and relaxing my cheeks I handed over some dollars. I noticed I got two bundles less than from the lift man but with my boyfriend standing looking over my shoulder I made no comment. He stayed with me throughout the transaction, then marched me back to where he'd found me. I wasn't sure whether a tip would be considered unlawful so I just said *Gracias* and *Adiós* seven or eight times. This seemed to do the trick as he pumped me heartily on the back and strode off.

I bought my plane tickets and was initiated in the South American game of 'No change'. Whatever the size of bank note you produce, shopkeepers will never have change to hand. The accessibility of change seems directly related to how much of a rush you're in. After ten minutes the little counter woman still hadn't returned from her search. I conceded victory, got on a likely looking plane and set off for São Paulo and Santa Cruz.

I was now flying some rubberband South American airway so I made sure I had a seat near the door. The plane was so empty that you could sit wherever you wanted. I was quite content with just the window in my escape hatch for company but unfortunately a large sweaty Bolivian woman took an interest in me. She placed a great variety of pot plants in the seat between us and demonstrated another South American game, 'Stare at the Foreigner'. I frequently caught her eyeing me through the fronds and vines. She proceeded to make rather a lot of bodily noises which reached a climax shortly after a very ugly stewardess had served some local delicacies. I was not very hungry although the stewardess gave me such an encouraging grin that her moustache touched her nose. To keep her happy I took a small brown battered ball from her proffered tray.

Under the breadcrumb crust it looked remarkably like a testicle. Unobserved I dropped it in the pot plants.

I couldn't make out much of the scenery below but it looked surprisingly barren. We landed at a tiny airport and I asked my pungent neighbour, 'Santa Cruz?'

'No.'

I must have pronounced Santa Cruz so correctly that she presumed I was fluent in Spanish. She took the opportunity to open the conversation. Every time she paused for breath I would say 'Mmm,' and nod my agreement or 'Mmm?' to show my surprise. After years of similar conversations with my mother, it was easy to guess the expected tone of my response, even if I didn't understand what she was saying. My 'Mmms' seemed to satisfy her and she nattered happily for a couple of hours.

While we were parked on the runway a baggage truck drove out from under the plane. Sitting on top of the cases I could clearly see my red and blue rucksack.

'Where the hell is that going?'

I stared after it, as it disappeared towards the terminal. My sleeping bag was not attached to it.

'Where the hell is my sleeping bag?'

I squashed my face against the reinforced plastic, trying to peep round the wing. A baggage handler walked out from under the plane. He was carrying my sleeping bag, but he was going the wrong way. I gestured desperately through the little window, 'You're going the wrong way!'

He trotted off oblivious of my considerate directions. I watched in frustrated impotence as my luggage vanished. I sat back and breathed deeply. There was nothing I could do but hope.

Fortunately my attention was diverted when two very attractive blonde-haired, blue-eyed girls got on the plane. Amazingly they were talking Spanish to each other. They looked like direct descendants of Hitler's youth. I later met some shaven-headed, blue-eyed eighty-year-old Germans, who said they had arrived in 1937 and were

Jewish. Klaus Barbie had lived for many years on the outskirts of Santa Cruz, working as an adviser to the Bolivian security forces.

When we arrived at Santa Cruz airport it was dark. I was greatly relieved to see I'd only lost my sleeping bag on the journey. I was now on auto-pilot. I hauled my bags out of the airport doors and breathed in my first real South American air. It was warm.

I read the name of a hotel to a taxi driver and I was whisked away through a blur of lights, unable to form any impresion. He dumped me at the hotel and bundled me out on the pavement. I stumbled in to the reception and said the phrase I had been practising for the last six thousand miles.

'*¿Tiene un habitacione simple por una noche?*'

'*No.*'

This wasn't the response in the 'Hotel' section of my phrase book. According to it the receptionist was supposed to say, 'Yes, sir, with or without a bathroom?'

I fell back on '*¿Habla Inglés?*'

'*No.*'

I discarded the phrase book and rummaged through my bag for my pocket dictionary. Were, what, when, where, where: *¿Dónde?*

'*¿Dónde habitacione?*'

She rang a neighbouring hotel and then pointed me in the right direction.

'*Gracias, Adiós.*'

I dragged my bags round the corner to the new hotel and tried again.

'*¿Tiene un habitacione simple por una noche?*'

'*Sí.*'

However, she didn't ask if I wanted with or without a bathroom. I told her anyway.

'*Con baño,*' my pronunciation sounding like a badly dubbed martial arts film.

'*Sí.*'

I booked in, was given a key, and directed to my room. The room was off a courtyard and the key opened the padlock bolted on the door. It was extremely basic but for five pounds a night it would have to do. I put my money under my pillow, bolted myself in and collapsed. I had been on the go for about forty hours, so within seconds I was asleep.

CHAPTER 4

*

Santa Cruz

I woke at nine the next morning and opened an anxious eyelid. From under the safety of my sheets I surveyed the room, which had a tiled floor, whitewashed walls and a broken electric fan. Propped up beside the bed was my large blue rucksack.

'Oh, God! I'm in Bolivia!'

I pushed back the sheets and checked the floor for scorpions before lowering my feet. To my surprise the room had an *en suite* bathroom minus the bath. I didn't fancy the shower as exposed wiring dangled dangerously along the rusty pipes. The cold water from the hot tap washed away any remnants of sleep. I unbolted my door and went out to discover South America.

At reception I booked in for another night and handed over my camera and binoculars to put in the safe. Then, clutching the map my father had given me, I peeped round the hotel door. A moment's hesitation before stepping out, then I was off, alone, a foreigner.

The first thing I noticed was the hexagonal slabs that interlocked to make the road surface. With tarmac always cracking in the heat, some bright spark had invented this method, which allowed for the great weather fluctuations. Squatting on tall curbs, the buildings were one storey high, square and whitewashed. Very few had windows, instead large shutters, which had now opened for the days' business. The streets had a vibrant energy as people rushed about desperate to complete their jobs before the oppressive midday heat.

I noticed two very distinctive races of people. Firstly there are the Camba, the people of Spanish descent. With tanned skin and brown hair, they are generally shorter than a European Spaniard. Many are very snobbish about trying to suggest they have untainted Spanish ancestry. The truth is that they are nearly all of mixed Indian and Spanish blood (*mestizo*) – the Spanish soldiers raped the Indian women for generations. The Camba are the ruling class in the state of Santa Cruz. They are famous for their parties and frivolity.

Then there are the Colla, pronounced Colyah, descendants of the Aymara and Quechuan Indians. The Aymara originate from the shores of Lake Titicaca in the northern Andes. They were fierce, fighting people that were never completely conquered by the huge might of the Inca Empire. The Quechuan were very much under the Inca umbrella and Quechua was the adopted language of the Incas.

Although in some towns of the Bolivian highlands the Quechuan and Aymara are still independent of each other, down in Santa Cruz they are all bracketed Colla. Colla was one of the original Aymara tribes but now the term is used disrespectfully to mean 'colonizers'. The Colla have been forced by government policy to leave the mountains and inhabit the sparsely populated lowlands around Santa Cruz.

The Colla are classic mountain people, sturdy and barrel-chested, to hold lungs large enough to cope with the thin high-altitude air. Their faces appear chiselled, with heavy features, prominent cheek bones, strong jawbones and hooked, flared noses. They are generally shorter than the Camba, averaging only about five feet. This is a result of a very poor mountain diet. Down in the lowlands every generation is already growing taller.

The women are squat, a shape which they accentuate to comical proportions with layer after layer of multicoloured skirts. Their skirts are a remnant of the rule of the Conquistadors. When the Conquistadors arrived they found the Indians wearing classic practical, peasant clothes. The women wore sensible and simple, long dresses. The Conquistadors decided they looked scruffy so they ordered the women to wear clothes modelled on the Spanish army drummer-boy uniform with flared pantaloons. This has been modified over the years into knee-length, brightly-coloured petticoats and skirts.

The women grow their hair down past their waist. They wear it in a single large plait while working and two plaits while socializing. They tie the plait up with brightly embroidered materials.

Without exception the Camba and Colla don't intermingle. The racial prejudice of the Camba is so extreme and ingrained that they barely acknowledge the existence of the Colla. They consider them lower than dogs. The situation is completely reversed in La Paz, where the Colla dominate. I later asked some Camba why they detested the Colla. I was told that it was because they were poor, dull, ignorant peasants.

When I pointed out that Westerners had more money than the Camba but I didn't consider myself superior, they countered that the Colla did everything differently. When asked for specific examples, they come up with: they kill a chicken differently, they slit its throat, we break its neck; they eat an orange differently, we chop it into pieces, they peel it in one long circular peel and then suck it.

I stepped carefully along the crowded streets, between the Colla street vendors, their selections of razors, mirrors and combs strewn across the pavement. I was heading towards the ODA office where my father had worked. The amount of interest I created was an indication of the rarity of Westerners. People kept trying to guide me but their directions proved incomprehensible so I just smiled politely and went on my way.

Santa Cruz was originally founded in 1561 by Spaniards

from Paraguay. It has boomed in the last thirty years and
is now an extremely affluent city of about six hundred
thousand people, making it Bolivia's second largest, after
La Paz in the highlands. The official reason for its new-
found wealth is the three or four small oil and gas fields
around it. But the real money comes from cocaine. Along
with Colombia, Bolivia is the world leader in cocaine
production. It is impossible to overestimate the power and
resources cocaine has brought to Santa Cruz.

I heard a rumour that one of the top drug barons, who
in Bolivia are called '*Pichegeteros*' (something to do with
willies), tried to make a deal with the Bolivian government.
He offered to pay off their six billion dollar national debt
if they legalized the export of cocaine. This rumour was
never substantiated but I do know the *Pichegeteros* build
towns for their workers in remote areas, complete with
hospitals, schools and churches. They are the real power
in this area and can dictate almost all events.

I was finding it very easy to navigate as the city is built
on a very simple design. There is a large central plaza and
from here fan the main streets in a block system. There
are two boundary roads that circle the city which on the
map are wider than the other roads.

The ODA office was on the inner circular. I found
the neat brick building and went in to introduce myself.
Fortunately they could speak English and they recognized
the family resemblance straight away. From there I rang
the National Park telephone number.

The Amboro office and headquarters were in a little
town sixty kilometres outside Santa Cruz called Buena
Vista. I got through almost immediately and spoke for the
first time to Robin Clarke. I had arrived a day early and
he was not at all pleased.

Before I left England I had managed to get a message
through to him of my arrival time in Rio de Janeiro.
Apparently Guy, the English volunteer, was waiting for
me at the airport, as they had found out when the next

plane from Rio came in. I hadn't expected anyone to meet me. The ODA ladies phoned the airport and paged Guy. I apologized about the mix-up and we agreed that I should meet him there as it was on the way to Buena Vista. I thanked the ladies and retraced my steps back to the hotel. Apart from this minor hiccup everything was moving remarkably smoothly.

At the hotel with the use of sign language I was told that the lady with the safe key had gone out for the day and wouldn't be back until late that afternoon. I swore and cursed at the timid receptionist but she shrugged, demonstrating her impotence. I marched back round to the ODA and explained my predicament. They rang the hotel and swore at the receptionist in Spanish. This was clearly a skill I should learn as soon as possible. They then organized a lift back to the hotel, a message announcing my delay to Guy and also a lift to the airport. I felt totally mothered. I thanked them profusely, collected my gear from the safe woman who had miraculously appeared and set off for the airport.

Things seemed to be happening far too fast and I was a little annoyed to be going straight to Buena Vista. A couple of days acclimatizing in Santa Cruz had appealed to me.

On the road back to the airport I had my first real look at the scenery. The land was totally flat and the Colla stood at every place a car may be forced to stop, selling oranges, cigarettes and biscuits. There were also a large number of people selling tickets for the national sport, lotto. Although empty, the airport was very clean and modern, built as a goodwill gesture by the Japanese only ten years before.

I spotted Guy as the only other Westerner in the airport. He was almost a caricature of my image of a field biologist. Medium height, shaggy hair, shaggy beard and shaggy clothes. He seemed remarkably laid back as he had been waiting for me for about three hours. We took a taxi to Montero, which is a medium-sized farming town half way between Santa Cruz and Buena Vista. It is the largest cocaine production area in the State of Santa Cruz.

The road quickly deteriorated outside the airport and very soon we were driving on nothing more than a wide dust track. The land viewed from the road seemed generally to be used for grazing cattle. These were Brahman cattle originally imported from India for their sturdiness. They are thin, creamy brown, with large horns and a big hump above their shoulders. Nearly all carried an impudently perched cattle egret. This white bird looks very like a heron. It eats the ticks and other parasites the cattle attract. Large black birds swirled high in the thermals above us.

'They're turkey vultures,' Guy informed, as matter of fact as a bank statement.

'Oh,' trying to sound equally nonchalant but not carrying it off.

As the car meandered around the crater-sized potholes, Guy explained the park set-up to me.

About seven years ago, Robin, while working for the ODA in Santa Cruz, had taken several trips into a largely unexplored area called Amboro. There he had caught a glimpse of a large wild turkey he identified as the horned curassow (*crax unicornis*), so named because of a blue horn protruding from its forehead. This bird had last been sighted in 1947 and was thought to be extinct. Greatly excited by this and also horrified by the rate of deforestation, he had been driven in his hope of making the area a national reserve.

The Bolivian government had not dismissed his idea but had given him little encouragement. Therefore with his own funds he dedicated himself to lobbying and pressurizing until the park was officially opened in 1984. It is an area the size of Wales and Robin was given an annual budget of five thousand dollars. Although the official boundaries were created, there was very little other change. Without the infrastructure to enforce the conservation, people were still felling the trees and hunting the animals.

To say the park was run on a shoestring would be an overstatement – more like a frayed piece of cotton.

Guy had met Robin a couple of years before while backpacking. He had returned to England and while finishing his degree had organized an expedition. Valerie, a genetics students, had also become involved and they raised enough sponsorship money to enable them to join Robin for a year. The work I would be helping them with was the general logging of the flora and fauna of the park and in particular we would study the horned curassow. The ornithological world was still sceptical of its existence and so our job was to produce information and photographs of it. If we could get world wildlife groups involved, then perhaps with their funds we could make this an effective conservation area.

I asked what had been achieved so far. Robin had been logging the birds for the last seven years, and with the help of Val and Guy over the last few months they had positively identified four hundred and sixty species of birds. They'd also discovered a few square kilometres of almost inaccessible mountain jungle where the curassow call could be heard regularly. Although Valerie had not yet seen the bird, Guy had managed to catch fleeting glimpses on three or four occasions.

My mind boggled. They had spent eight months, day in day out, looking for this whopping great turkey and Valerie still hadn't seen it. It came as no surprise to me that the world still believed it extinct. They had no idea of the number of curassows as they had only been located by chance and were not known to exist in any other part of the world. There may be no more than a dozen birds alive.

*

By the time all this had been explained we had arrived at Montero. It had the same layout as Santa Cruz with a central plaza and block system. I noticed a couple of Japanese men walking out of a shop and Guy explained that there was a large Japanese Okinawese colony on the outskirts of the town. They had left the Japanese island of Okinawa at the end of the Second World War, afraid of American occupation, and had sailed from country to country, searching for a new home. They had been turned away from all, until Bolivia allowed them in. Now firmly established, they grow cotton, sugar, rice and coffee with the usual Japanese efficiency.

We didn't stay long and I was told that the final leg of our journey would be by Micro, a special four-wheel-drive bus. It was my initiation to typical Bolivian travel. A small bus with only about twenty seats, the wheels are disproportionately large to cope with the non-existent road surface. We were fortunate to get seats as the thirty-kilo-metre ride takes well over an hour. The driver only set off when he'd packed in as many people as possible, complete with their bags of rice and live chickens. The driver's console was reassuringly surrounded with drawings and plastic statues of Christ and the Madonna. I hoped this devoutness was not indicative of the journey.

The bus was incredibly cramped and, although the door was left open, the lack of ventilation sent the temperature soaring. The dust road became ever more potholed and, with the cranking of gears and clamour of the engine, conversation was impossible. I decided to take in the view.

The fields took on a slightly less organized appearance but the panorama was still boringly flat and treeless. Guy, seated behind, patted my shoulder and pointed out some very distant mountain peaks. 'Amboro,' he shouted. As we crossed the bridge of yet another incredibly wide river, which could only be described as a flood plain, Amboro started to take shape. Although still a distance away, I could only get a vague impression of the size of this

National Park. A few minutes later Guy pointed to a church tower protruding up from behind a hill.

'Buena Vista.'

Chapter 5

*

Buena Vista

The bus left the main track and headed up the hill on the approach road to Buena Vista. The poverty came as a bit of a surprise after the almost European Santa Cruz. All the buildings in Buena Vista are one storey except the priest's house. They are almost mostly adobe huts, feeble consructions of latticed wood covered in mud. The road was deeply rutted and emaciated dogs were chased by half-dressed urchins.

As we came on to the plaza it was the lack of life which made such an impression. It was a ghost town. We were the only two passengers to get off and we had to scramble over the sacks. The Micro drove off, tooting its goodbyes, the occupants staring at us and the braver ones actually waving. I waved back, which created a great cheer as they disappeared round the bend. Silence enveloped us. Buena Vista was quieter than a church mouse wearing slippers.

We stood on a cobbled road, surrounded by my collection of bags and breathed in the sights.

'Oh dear,' was my reaction.

The road confined the central square of squat, bulbous-trunked trees. Dominating the plaza and taking up almost all of one side, was a red-stoned church with a crumbling bell tower. Flanking the plaza on all other sides was a two-feet-high pavement with long, uniform one-storey buildings. The buildings looked like stables, complete with two-piece doors and wooden shutters. Apart from the church and adjacent priest's house, the square was totally symmetrical.

Guy led me down to one of the few open doorways. A small wooden plaque announced it as the Amboro National Park office. Inside it looked like an empty coal shed. The only furnishings were two desks and a lightbulb. The floor was uneven brick but someone had tried to brighten the patchy stone walls with wildlife posters.

I had now collected and analysed my first impressions and came to the conclusion that 'Oh dear,' was pretty accurate.

At the desk sat a very pretty young girl bashing ineffectively at a large antiquated typewriter. As we walked in she looked up shyly. I guessed she was about fourteen, which was rather a pity as she was almost beautiful. Guy introduced me to Charo. Unable to speak Spanish, I just smiled. Guy laughed and joked with her for a while and found out that Robin was at Pablo's bar.

I was greatly relieved to hear there was a bar. We set off to find him down a rutted sand track lined with adobe huts. The bar was just a two-roomed shed with a yard out the back. In one of the rooms lives the landlord, Pablo, his wife and four children. It's allowed to be called a bar because in the other room is a large stocked fridge and a bottle opener.

Robin, a sun-tanned Alex Higgins lookalike, was sitting alone on a plank of wood with only a bottle of beer for company. He shook my hand and told me to get a bottle of the local beer, Ducal. I followed Guy's example of helping myself to a bottle and glass from the fridge and joined Robin on his plank where he helped himself to my beer. We sat among the chickens and ducks drinking bottle after bottle. Nothing important was discussed: just my journey and the present situation in Buena Vista and Amboro. As night fell we watched the chickens climb into the trees to roost and the moths swarm around the one and only street light. Robin eventually stood up and told me to come to his house. He got on to his aged motorbike and I jumped on when he'd picked up speed. I was balanced rather precariously with my rucksack on my back. He told me, as we went along, that the bike had no brakes or clutch. I'd already noticed the complete lack of tread on the tyres and wished I'd had a few more beers. We drove along in the pitch black until we came to his one-roomed house. Guy sensibly followed on foot.

Robin and I chatted for about another half an hour about my contribution to their work. He didn't think I would have much time to follow my particular interest of herpetology as they were working almost exclusively on gathering information on the curassow. Virtually mid-sentence he got up and lay on his bed. Pulling off his shoes and socks, he turned to Guy and said, 'Get that needle on the shelf. I've got a chigger.'

'You want me to dig it out?'

'Of course I do.'

Robin gestured for me to move closer and said, 'You'd better watch this, Oliver. You're bound to get them.'

'Happy to, but – er – could you tell me what a chigger is?'

'Hurry up, Guy. Stick it in. Yes, it's a sand flea. You get them if you walk about barefoot.'

'I see, and what does it do?'

Guy selected a needle and gingerly prodded Robin's foot.

'It burrows under your skin and dies. Oooch! Shit! Be careful and don't burst it.'

'It dies . . .' I prompted.

'Yes and becomes a propagation sack for the eggs to hatch into maggots.'

'So what you've got in your foot is a bag of maggots.'

'No, you have to get them out before they hatch or else they start crapping and cause infection.'

Guy added, 'If you can imagine something itchier than the itchiest thing you can think of, well they're even itchier than that.'

'Pretty itchy, then?'

'Yep.' I started to wonder if they were both barking mad.

'Gotcha!'

'Ahhh! Did you get it?'

'Yeah, and it didn't burst.'

Guy offered me the needle with a speared bubble of fly eggs on its point.

'Umm, nice.'

Robin stood up and dropped his trousers.

'I'm going to bed. Go and sleep at Guy's.'

'Righty-ho.'

As we tramped along a sand track in the midnight blackness I wondered if this was typical for a day in Bolivia. Guy led me off the path into a field. Half obscured by the undergrowth, we found his hut, which he called the Whitehouse. Although he lit a candle for me I was too tired and drunk to comment on the decor. I stretched out on an old purple sofa and wrapped myself in a fine linen sheet used to disguise the sofa's colour. Nervous of vicious beasties, I curled up in the sheet and made sure everything was tucked in. Before you could say 'First-time buyer', I was dreaming contentedly of arranging a mortgage for a tree house.

I woke early next morning to find Guy already up. I was relieved the house was not a mud hut but a nice, two-roomed bungalow. The floor was tiled and the walls plastered. The smaller room was Valerie's bedroom and the other was the kitchen, dining room and Guy's bedroom. There was no electricity, hot water or carpets and there were a few too many cockroaches and spiders for my liking, but I was pleasantly surprised at the level of civilization.

Valerie was in the park with Clemente (one of the two park guards), so Guy and I had the opportunity to get to know each other. It became clear that he had not been consulted about my arrival, which had rather put his back up. He also considered the house too small for all three of us. He was extremely polite about this but I was getting rather angry about the lack of organization. After coming all this way I wasn't happy to be thought of as an encumbrance. But I was glad of the opportunity to get to know Guy without the presence of the zany vegetarian.

I still had three thousand dollars down my boxer shorts so I was eager to stow the crisp notes in a safe place before I developed a rash. Guy took me up to the plaza to introduce me to the priests and he told me to ask them to look after my money. They had the best security in the area as the local thieves either feared the wrath of God or they couldn't pick the safe.

We knocked on their door behind the church. I was introduced to Padre Paul and Dennis. Paul was an American in his fifties who had lived in Buena Vista for over twenty years. Dennis, also American, had just finished his degree in theology and was experiencing life as a missionary. He was spending the year in Buena Vista before deciding which religious order to join. Paul was happy to look after my money and they told me to visit when I'd settled in.

I decided to return to Santa Cruz to buy a sleeping bag so I walked back to the plaza and caught the next Micro back to Montero. No seats were available so I spent almost an hour and a half bent double.

From Montero I caught a Trufi, a communal taxi, three in the back and three in the front. I shared the front seat with a rotund lady of admirable proportions. Unfortunately her huge hips obstructed the gear stick so the car was stuck in third. However, with considerable contortions she rolled her weight on to me so the driver could slam the lever into fourth gear. Meanwhile I was squashed to the door by her mountainous bosom. Although I found an air pocket between her breasts it wasn't enough. Turning blue, I wound down the window and prised my head out into glorious freedom. Arriving in Santa Cruz slightly tyre-marked, it was getting late so I went and booked back into the hotel with the disappearing safe keys.

Early the next morning I went looking for the camping shops Guy had marked on my map. There were only two and the first had never even heard of sleeping bags. Fortunately the other shop had and I chose one from their extensive range of two.

Outside the camping shop a local strode up to me. I'd already noticed South Americans were particularly fond of asking foreigners the time, and I guessed by the purpose in his step that he was going to ask me something. I had just prepared the translation of ten past eleven when he spoke.

'Do you want to buy some cocaine?'

'Cocaine? Erm, no thank you.'

He nodded and walked away. I spent the rest of the morning buying food for our trip. I bought rice, tins of spam, sardines, a few packet soups and a large sheet of pink plastic to make a shelter as the park didn't run to spare tents. I changed a bit more money into the local currency, bolivianos, and set off back to Buena Vista.

Back at the Whitehouse, Valerie had returned from the park. She stood up and said, 'Hi, where's Robin?' This welcome proved to be just initial shyness, as we were soon chatting happily. I didn't think Valerie had any right to be shy as she was quite a stunner. She was tall, slim and with a sculptured beauty I would find difficult to avoid.

She had very kindly prepared a roast chicken and she explained that, although they tried to be vegetarian, it was almost impossible with the ingredients available in Buena Vista.

Sadly, the magnitude of this gesture escaped me at the time. There is no nipping down to the eight-till-late for an oven-ready chicken in Bolivia. You have to walk the village trying to persuade the locals that they can spare one. With much pleading and waving of bank notes, a local may agree. He then attempts to catch it. The term free-range takes on a new perspective as the convicted hen takes refuge in a banana plantation. The local enlists the support of the rest of his family. They take it in turns to chase the hen until it finally collapses from exhaustion. They then hand it to you. You hand it back and gesture that you want it dead. For several minutes they pretend ignorance in the hope of procuring a higher price. You eventually compromise and offer them a cigarette. You then discover that the entire family smokes, even the three-month-old baby. They break the chicken's neck and hand it over, still flapping. Their job is done; you, however, still have to pluck it, disembowel it and cook it.

We ate and drank a great deal that evening and I retired to my sofa well puffed. I woke up late the next morning feeling a little groggy due to the evening's excesses. I sat up on the sofa in a confused morning-after state and tried to work out in which order I should put on my clothes.

After a couple of minutes of indecision I went for order of accessibility. Only one sock was visible and as finding the other would involve premature departure from my sitting position I decided to go without. My eyelids were already drooping after this prolonged exertion. I reached for my shoes and lazily tried to wriggle my foot in. My bare toes touched something cold and clammy. I sprang up, jerking my foot out of the shoe and screamed. Jumping from one foot to the other, as one does when freshly arrived from suburban England and confronted with unimaginable horrors in one's shoe, I noticed that Valerie and Guy were watching my movements with amused curiosity. Not wishing to appear a complete idiot I attempted to pass off my behaviour as some sort of early morning exercise routine. I did a couple of bends and stretches to emphasize the point.

As they appeared unimpressed, I gave up the charade and set about investigating my footwear. I picked up the broom and bravely gave the shoe a nudge. Nothing happened. I nudged it again and leapt on to the sofa when a dark shape appeared from within. A large green tree frog stuck out his head to see what was causing the commotion. Deciding there was no peace to be had, he hauled himself out of the shoe and ambled across the floor, out through the open door and into the garden. Fortunately I have the ability to laugh at myself. This came in very handy as the story was re-enacted for everyone's benefit on many occasions over the next few days.

I decided to take the accommodation problem into my own hands. Armed with a phrase book, I went off to find a place of my own. I'd been told which house belonged to the local amateur estate agent and so I shook the curtain draped over her doorway. She led me to the infant school behind the church where I was offered a completely bare room off the school yard. The window was broken and the brick walls were covered in cobwebs. There was no furniture whatsoever. I was not impressed so she started the hard sell. She told me I could use the school bathroom, a room very similar to the bedroom but with a concrete urinal, a cold-water shower, and freefall hole-in-the-ground toilet. I asked if she had anything else.

I was given a despairing, '*Si.*'

The woman was quite baffled that I didn't want this top-of-the-range property. As she marched back to the plaza I prayed for something a little better. She showed me a room off the plaza, almost next to the Amboro office. I would have the entire place to myself. The walls were plastered and the floor tiled. I could also take a bed from the storeroom. The bathroom was clean and had a light-bulb. I said I would take it. We agreed on a price of sixty dollars a month, although she couldn't rent it indefinitely. We spent the next hour trying to get the electricity put on. As there were no sockets all this effort was for my solitary lightbulb. I selected a bed without any obvious animal inhabitants and looked forward to my inde-pendence. I walked back down to the Whitehouse to collect my gear.

It was getting late and as I had no food or cooking utensils I was persuaded to stay for a vegetable curry. By the time it was prepared and eaten I didn't fancy lumping all my gear back up to the plaza so I stayed the night. Bright and early the next morning, at about twelve, I started carrying my bags up to my unfurnished adobe apartment. I was just passing Robin's house when he intercepted me and sat on the road for a chat. He wanted me to stay at the Whitehouse.

He explained that generally there are only two sorts of foreigners in Bolivia. The first are missionaries and the second are involved in the cocaine industry. Even after all this time, he still had to justify his presence to the Bolivians. Many didn't believe his reasons for going into the jungle. They thought he had his own coca cultivation plots or he was searching for gold. It was simply beyond their comprehension that he was looking at birds. To enforce conservation in Amboro we had to be incredibly brutal. Forcing peasant farmers off the land was the only way to stop them chopping down the forest. Everybody connected with Amboro was therefore hated by some of the locals. In the early days of Amboro a peasant lynch-mob had threatened to hang Robin and these groups still look for any excuse to cause political trouble for Amboro. My living on my own up at the plaza was open to misinterpretation. I needed to be seen to be totally integrated into the park staff.

I had only been there three days and didn't want to rock the boat so I turned round and headed back to the Whitehouse. My return was not greeted favourably but I was too fed up to care. I unpacked my bag and got ready to go into the Amazon rainforest the next day.

CHAPTER 6

Amboro

At eight the next morning we were given a lift to the edge of the park. We bounced around in the back of a four-wheel-drive pick-up as it scattered the vagrant cows from the sand road. Four vultures flapped off in front of us, leaving a dog's rotted carcass for later consumption. We drove on for just under an hour to reach a small collection of huts called Terminal, which is the last legal civilization before entering the park. The natural boundary is a river called the Surutu. We climbed from the truck and walked through a gap in the palm trees on to a huge sandy beach. It was about two or three hundred metres across. It looked like the Mediterranean.

We walked to the water and to my surprise Valerie and Guy just waded in. It was deceptively shallow and didn't come above my waist. When we reached the other side my waterpoof boots had about half a pint of water in each. After a hundred metres of slooshing along, I swopped them for my track shoes. With no pretence for water resistance they let the water out as easily as they let it in.

One problem in Amboro is the campesino families that are illegally farming in the park. They are gradually slashing and burning further and further into the reserve. Some of them have turned away from the subsistence farming of rice and yucca. In the seclusion of the park they have been tempted to grow coca. Although this is a traditional Bolivian crop used by the locals to deaden hunger, it is also used in the production of cocaine.

Following the path we passed many of these small-holdings. We stopped at a particularly wealthy farm known to possess two horses and we hired the animals to carry our bags. For the next twenty minutes we tried to tie four unevenly weighted rucksacks to two semi-wild horses but with no saddles to attach them to, the bags slipped off every few miles. To stop the horses running back to their field we had to walk behind them, cutting off their retreat with large sticks. We followed the path past three or four other small farms.

The horses finally accepted their burdens and Valerie waited with them while Guy led me off the path to meet Clemente, the park guard.

We walked from the trees into a sun-baked clearing. A twenty-foot-long palm hut defied gravity and architectural conventions. It was partitioned into two rooms: one room was the bedroom and the other the living area. There were no doors and the living area's outside walls were only half the height of the roof. This was to allow the smoke from the open fire to escape.

We found Clemente in the front room enjoying his only luxury, a small transistor radio. With a bent length of wire as an aerial and the batteries fading rapidly, the reception was crackly and barely audible. But he sat with his ear pressed against it, a contented smile on his wide mouth.

He was a tiny man of about five feet with a very round and comical face. He wore a green bobble hat which I never saw him without. He was quite dwarfed by his wife who was as wide as he was tall. She bustled about her household tasks, controlling and disciplining her five young children with infinite patience.

Clemente was considered by his neighbours to be a wealthy man. He had a steady income from the park and he owned a horse. He lived in this hut with his wife and large brood all sharing the same bamboo bed. The children didn't go to school because, even if they could have afforded the fees, the nearest one was twenty kilometres away in Buena Vista. They spent the day chasing the chickens and fetching water from the river.

As soon as he saw us he jumped up. Guy introduced me and I was amazed as Clemente greeted me. His voice was a deep baritone, incredibly rich and musical. In England I've no doubt he could have earned a fortune doing the voice overs for margarine adverts, especially if he could have faked an Irish accent. Unfortunately I was still unable to say more than *Buenas tardes* (Good afternoon). I said it anyway, disregarding the fact it was morning.

Clemente had been a hunter until a year ago and so he had the best qualifications for park guard. He'd spent his entire forty-odd years living in or on the edge of the jungle. In his last months as a hunter he'd stolen eggs from a razor-billed curassow nest. A close relation of the horned curassow, it is a large, heavily-bodied bird with black feathers and white tips to its tail. He had kept them hoping to hatch and keep them as pets. Robin spotted the chicks while recruiting Clemente to work for the park and ordered their protection for the interest of any visiting ornithologists. It gave me an idea of what we were looking for.

We left Clemente to his radio and rejoined the path. Shortly after leaving we sighted the last and biggest farm. This was owned by the Arnaldos. As we walked along Guy warned me about Mrs Arnaldo. 'She's mad.' He wouldn't elaborate. It was therefore with slight apprehension that I approached a distant figure waving to us from the doorway of a large hut.

As we drew closer no explanation was necessary. A woman of about fifty stood in an evening gown and wellingtons against the background of a mud hut and the Amazon rainforest. Guy introduced me and I was forced to kiss her smeared face. I offered her a cigarette and she took two for later. Guy explained we had much work to do and we quickly escaped. She stood waving goodbye as we tramped on.

Eventually we found ourselves on another wide river and I knelt down on the sand to take a drink before continuing. Bending over the shallow water with my hands cupped to drink, I noticed a small fish, about an inch long. It trod water against the current, remaining stationary under a small clump of reed.

I remained motionless and my patience was rewarded as it flitted out from under the reed, stopping abruptly in my shadow, only inches from my face. I recognized the jerky way it swam, its size and shape, the red and blue speckles on its gold body and most noticeably the sharp black front-edge to its dorsal fin. It was unmistakable. It was a Ramírez's dwarf cichlid.

I was totally chilled out at this momentous experience. I looked up to beckon Guy and Valerie so that they could share in this stunning field identification. They hadn't waited and were already thirty metres up the river. I was horrified. I needed to share this moment. I had no one to instruct about the dwarf cichlid's short lifespan and fierce territorial habits, its scavenger tendencies and preference for the bottom of slow-moving shallow rivers. I could even have told him that a Ramírez dwarf cichlid cost two pounds fifty down at Abdul's Aquatics in Grosvenor Street.

On reflection, I decided not to call Guy and Valerie as I was uncertain they would share my passion for dwarf cichlids. I stayed watching my little aquatic chum until the fear of losing them finally overcame me and I dragged myself off in pursuit. I caught up, puffing and panting. Guy eyed me quizzically, the excitement and enthusiasm still evident on my face. I skipped alongside him, my fatigue forgotten.

'I've just seem a Ramírez dwarf cichlid!' I blurted, not able to wait for the question. He looked at me sceptically without breaking stride.

'It's a fish,' I groaned, exasperated at the solitude of genius.

'Oh, nice,' he walked on, his mind now elsewhere.

I stood staring at his back like a child whose dream
toy has been trashed only three days after Christmas. I
trudged after him pouting grumpily. We walked for the
rest of the day and although I managed to recite my cichlid
encounter to both of them in more detail, I never received
the slightest enthusiastic response.

Late in the afternoon we came out of the jungle and
crossed a river where above the bank we found a small
wooden shack. I was delighted to have reached that day's
destination and I collapsed. After hanging up my mosquito
net, we all went down to the stream for a swim.

A rockfall had created a green-tinged clear lagoon. Guy
and Valerie stripped with all the modesty of hardened
naturists. Maybe Bolivia had liberated them but I was a
new boy. Nakedness was not English, it was embar-
rassingly continental, Scandinavian even. Standing, white
as a milk bottle in my baggy boxer shorts, I goggled as
they let their bits hang free. Fortunately they plunged into
the pool, the water clouding their boldness.

I took off my socks and stood at the water's edge,
dunking my toe. The sandflies were having a field-day,
biting my prudish flesh. Oh, what the hell! I've played
rugby. I peeled off civilization, subconsciously shielding
my sun-shy privates by scratching a convenient itch on
my leg. I stepped into the water and disappeared. In my
haste I had not noticed how deep it was.

I came spluttering to the surface, but now with my
virtues camouflaged I relaxed and wallowed in luxury.

'This is fantastic,' I enthused.

'Yes,' responded the veterans, busy with the soap.

I sploshed around, floating my legs in a very passable
impression of a Canadian logging trawler. I chugged on
contentedly until I noticed I had drifted into dark water.
The anonymous depths persuaded me to propel my paddle
barge into turbo. When I regained the shallows, Guy said,
'You have to be careful in these pools. We don't stay in
too long.'

'Why's that, Guy?' I said, faking unconcern.

'Well, there's a minuscule fish that lives in these rivers. It's so small that it can swim up any orifice.'

'Really,' I sneered.

'Yes, last year a man had to have half his willy chopped away to get a fish out.'

'Yeah, sure,' I scoffed, while I surreptitiously squeezed the tip of my precious appendage. Guy laughed and stepped out of the pool.

'Believe what you want.'

I followed after a resolute ten seconds. Refreshed, we had begun to collect water and firewood when a young boy walked into our camp to collect the horses. He looked so disgustingly fresh after his journey that I felt like removing his grin with a large spiky club. Instead we gave him a mug of coffee into which he shovelled the standard Bolivian ration of sugar, about six heaped spoonfuls. They were dessert spoons. He swilled it down and sprung up on to one of the horses. Throwing a rope round the other horse's neck he beat his mount into action with a stick and was soon out of sight down the path.

It was dark before we had cooked our meal of sardines and rice; the first meal of the day. I was so exhausted that I only gave my Ramírez cichlid story one more go, still with no response. I consoled myself that in the world of cichlids they were both Philistines. Despite the hardness of the ground, I quickly fell asleep and dreamed that I was being bitten by my watery pal. I woke during one particularly aggressive attack to find dozens of ants nibbling me contentedly. Also, in my slumbering combat I must have struck out, as my mosquito net had slipped, allowing in hungry mosquitos.

Early the next morning, after brewing coffee, we set off. My feet were already blistered, my neck sunburnt and I was stiff all over. I faced the day with trepidation. I was told there were no more wide paths and so with my heavy rucksack it was going to be rough. There were no further signs of humanity as we entered the jungle. Apparently we were following a path but I could see no evidence of it. The trees became steadily larger and the most common was a species of ficus which has huge buttress roots. We saw no animals but we could hear birds screeching overhead, flying above the canopy. It was dank and dark.

We were forced to bridge a swamp by walking along a huge fallen tree and Guy passed back advice as he led the procession. 'Watch you don't slip off, this place is full of snakes.'

'Righty-ho, Guy, will do.' The advice continued as we clambered down a slippery mud bank.

'Watch out for the Armadillo holes.'

'OK, no problem.'

We tramped on, stepping carefully betwen Armadillo burrows while flocks of blue-headed parrots swooped and screeched above us. These parrots are confusingly named, for their most distinctive feature is their red tails.

Guy and Valerie were both cucumber cool, while I fought desperately to keep the excitement off my face.

We hiked steadily uphill, the forest becoming dense as the ferns and small palms spread in the gaps between the trees. It soon became almost impenetrable and so we pushed our way through to a river. It was a relief to be in the open again and I drank gratefully before setting off up the riverbed.

It was flat for the first few miles and I was able to take in the scenery. Around every bend there was a stunning new view. Although the river was shallow it had formed deep clear pools with sharp cliffs and the forest rose away steeply. Huge trees lined the banks, covered in moss, orchids and tarzan vines. Palms and ferns of all sizes and shapes grew in profusion. The temperature well into the eighties and the intense humidity forced us to rest frequently.

I spotted prints in the riverbed and identified the tapir with its heavy, three-toed impression. There were also deer tracks, small cat prints and running alongside the river for quite a few kilometres were large cat prints, as big as my hand. They were either puma or jaguar and I decided to study the plaster of Paris prints in the Amboro office more vigorously before the next visit. The only life we saw were birds and butterflies. Huge morpho butterflies with electric-blue wings swooped around us, smaller red and orange heliconid butterflies fluttered to land on the sand banks to lick up the salt. While resting, foolhardy butterflies occasionally landed on my hand, to lap up my sweat for the salt it contained.

The most evident bird was the crested orapendola. Looking vaguely like a crow, except for a yellow head and tail, it can mimic the call of most other forest birds. This bird is every ornithologist's nightmare, as it has at least thirty of its own calls before you count its ability to mimic. Tropical birds only have a twenty-five per cent breeding success rate. The orapendolas, however, are extremely successful. They nest in colonies of about a dozen. They weave a long dangling basket nest, which they suspend like Christmas stockings from the very outer branches of high trees. They thus take safety in numbers and are also almost inaccessible to even the most determined snakes. Their biggest predators are flies which lay eggs on the baby orapendolas. The maggots hatch and crawl down the chicks' nostrils and start eating them from inside. The orapendolas combat these flies by nesting in the same tree as wasps or bees. These kill all other insects and so keep the flies away.

The river started to rise steeply and, with mounting fatigue, I lost all interest in the scenery and gritted my teeth just to survive the journey. After clambering over progressively larger boulders for about five hours, I was ready to collapse. Fortunately we arrived at the study area base camp. We'd been wading, climbing, scrambling and jumping for approximately six hours that day and seven hours the day before. My feet were agony.

The base camp was just a flat sand bank on the river. I didn't have a tent so I built a shelter with my mosquito net shrouded by a plastic sheet. Although there were still a couple of hours of daylight, I was in no mood to look for a bloody turkey. I was grateful that Valerie seemed equally worn out. We went for another dip in the river and then cooked the food.

So far the only contact I'd had with the local fauna was with the insects. The mosquitos could bite through shirts and even canvas trousers. There were tiny flies called inhenies that were invisible until they bit you. You'd feel a sharp prick and look down horrified, expecting to find a huge killer wasp, but you would see nothing. On closer inspection you would notice a tiny black speck. Despite squashing the insect the area would swell and redden. They never made any attempt to fly off. It seemed that the only ambition these kamikazi insects had was to cause pain. Once this was delivered they were happy to die.

This was only my second day in the jungle and I was already having insecticide fantasies, everything from fly swats to napalm. I looked as if I'd just had a bad case of chicken pox. The previous evening in the comparative safety of my sleeping bag I inspected my body, only to find somewhere along the way I'd picked up several ticks. These are the most disease-ridden insects known to man. They carry everything. Fortunately in this area they lived mainly on tapirs. This meant they carried tapir diseases and were not particularly dangerous to us.

The ticks bury their heads in your skin and suck up blood, filling their flat bodies until after only a few days they swell up to many times their original size. It seemed that they were digging in faster than I could pull them out. Sometimes the larger ones embed their heads so firmly in your skin that any attempt to remove them would decapitate them. Their heads would then have to be dug out leaving an extremely infected sore.

While our pot of sardines and rice simmered away, I

smoked at least ten cigarettes and swiped constantly at the clouds of insects. Darkness brought slight relief from all except the mosquitos, who had their own efficient blood radar. We kipped early, setting the large alarm clock for five-thirty.

At two in the morning a storm hit us, wrecking my makeshift shelter. The plastic sheeting was torn from its achors. I was soaked and spent the rest of the night curled shivering in the last two feet of dryish sleeping bag holding the plastic in position above my head. Despite these hardships the adventure of being in the Amazon was keeping me going and I got up with the light still feeling fresh.

I walked off a little way down the river to relieve myself. Climbing the bank I went a few yards into the jungle and with a machete I made my own dugout privy.

I had my trousers round my ankles when I heard the rustling of leaves. It was so close and distinct that my bowels reacted immediately. From my squatting position I searched for the source of the noise. The rustling came from on top of a rock ledge and was now even louder. My frozen panic was shattered by the snap of a twig.

It's a jaguar!

Clutching my trousers I jumped up. They snagged on a treeroot. Anchored, half naked, to the ground, I was as sacrifical as any Old Testament lamb. A pounce seemed imminent.

I yanked desperately at my tethered trousers. They came free, pitching me forward. Stumbling, I snatched at a small tree. Pulling myself upright, a shadow formed on the ridge and let out two chesty cough-like barks.

He was a hungry jaguar!

Stabilized against the tree, two sharp points of agonizing pain scored simultaneous hits on the back of my hand and seared up my arm. The shock loosened my grip on the trousers and they slid back down. Clutching my injured hand I hopped out into the open as fast as my constricting trousers would allow, my white buttocks bouncing like two succulent rump steaks. With space available, I covered my vulnerables and, adequately decent, I turned to face my aggressor.

The rustling grew fainter and moved away up into the jungle. Reasonably satisfied that I would face no further attack from the pussycat, I looked down at my hand, fearing the worst. True enough there were two punctures, but instead of fragments of snake fang, there were two small red ants with their jaws still locked into my flesh.

They were palacanthia ants, so called because they live in a symbiosis with the palacanthia tree. The tree supplies them with habitat and a tasty sap and in return they fiercely protect the tree from animal and insect attack. They also eat away a circle round the tree to protect it from saplings or vines that might challenge its space. The little tree is extremely straight, fiercely untouchable and surrounded by a halo of bare earth. It is therefore known locally as *palosanto* (sainted pole), from which palacanthia has been derived.

The ant bites are so intensely painful that the insects are shipped to North American medical institutes for use in the treatment of arthritis. They need no provocation to bite and their poison is supposed to work as an inflammation alleviator for the swollen joints of arthritis sufferers.

They made my entire hand numb. Feeling rather foolish I brushed them off and walked briskly back to camp. The hairs on the back of my neck tingling, I couldn't help checking over my shoulder every few steps for signs of further attack.

Guy was sitting by the fire busy making coffee. I mentioned the sounds I'd heard rather matter-of-factly. He looked in the direction I indicated and said nervously, 'That's the sound a jaguar makes.'

I'd already come to this conclusion but faced with confirmation I didn't want to draw further attention to my dangerous behaviour. I'd roused Mr Jaguar from his post-meal slumber and he was just annoyed to be disturbed. If he'd wanted to eat me I'm sure I would never have heard him.

After coffee, Guy and I went off to search for the turkey. We left the river and climbed up into the jungle fighting our way through thickets and barbed vines. As we walked through a dark, swampy clearing, I was a few steps behind when directly in front of me I noticed a large, blue-grey snake, curled and ready to strike. Its mouth was badly misshapen. Guy must have stood on its head. Faced with my first proper field identification, I was completely flummoxed and, after photographing it, we let it glide off over the watery swamp.

Carrying on up the steepening slope we came to the base of the huge cliffs that are visible thirty kilometres back in Buena Vista. These cliffs form an impentrable barrier that protects the heart of the park. To the best of local knowledge, no one had ever been past them. We walked parallel with the cliffs until we came out at a clearing. A beautiful waterfall plummeted a hundred feet, crashing on to a huge rock-fall at the cliff base. As we walked out into the sunshine Guy spotted a shape halfway up a tree. Sitting motionless was a tamandor, a furry little anteater about the size of a small dog. Its golden brown fur has black stripes and it has a surprisingly short muzzle for an anteater. Unable to move fast, it just sat in the tree posing for photographs. We eventually left it in peace and went to explore the waterfall.

The water had worn a spout in the cliff top which funnelled the cascade away from the vertical edge so it dropped in one unbroken stream. Hundreds of brightly coloured teeid lizards zipped between the boulders. I climbed to the top of the rock-fall and stood in the spray rainbows, breathless at the view. There were two levels of cliff and these were just the first. They walled in the valley on three sides. The river we had followed was the only way to enter the valley. Beyond the second range of cliffs lay virgin forest.

After an hour sitting around taking in the scenery, we set off back for camp. Guy stopped me frequently, asking, 'Did you hear that?' I would shake my head dumbly.

'That's the horned curassow,' he would say.

It rained again that night and looked as if it was going to set in for the next few days. With the rain, visibility fell from poor to almost nil. The decision was made to return to Buena Vista.

Before eight in the morning we packed up camp and set off. The going was a great deal easier as it was much simpler to clamber downriver than it was to climb up. The rucksacks were also a great deal lighter as we had left the remaining cans of food for a future visit.

We walked all day reaching the little village, Terminal, at six o'clock. We had stopped only for short fag breaks. There was no vehicle to meet us but fortunately we caught a lift in the back of a dying lorry. It had been made in the 1950s and was kept together by planks of wood, lengths of rope and a great deal of prayer.

Back at the Whitehouse I went to bed. Actually I went to sofa but it was luxury and I slept a dead man's sleep.

CHAPTER 7

*

Yuqui Indians

Back in Buena Vista I rested. Valerie went off down to Santa Cruz to collect the mail. My clothes were taken by our cleaner to be scrubbed by hand in her wheelbarrow. A wheelbarrow was considered a modern appliance, in contrast to the standard method of beating clothes on the rocks down at the river. Not one person in Buena Vista owned a washing machine.

We paid our cleaner twelve pounds a month plus benefits. Twelve pounds was considered a generous wage but I subsidized it by giving her the odd windfallen mango from the garden.

Guy and I spent the time building a chicken house round the side of the Whitehouse. The chickens had taken to sleeping huddled together on the front porch. Every morning on awakening we would walk barefoot on to the porch to breathe in the day. This experience would be somewhat spoiled by standing in chicken shit. The chickens were being steadily picked off by a variety of snakes, wild cats and opossums that lived in our roof. We also believed they were disappearing into our neighbour's pot but we were never able to prove it. We agreed it would be safer for them to spend the night off the ground in a house. We spent many hours trying to train them to sleep in it. We coaxed them using corn trails leading them to the hutch. Eventually we just chased them around and then stuffed them forcibly in, standing guard at the entrance. The second we left, however, they would jump out and toddle on round to sit on the porch. I recommended that we just cooked them. Guy was for the idea but said that unfortunately they were Valerie's pride and joy. We continued their fruitless training.

Robin had decided that it was time to build a permanent base in the study area. It was arranged that we should meet Estaban, the other park guard, to start work on a hut. While arranging the details, Estaban had given Robin the report of his last patrol. Only a few kilometres from our study area he had found human tracks on a river bank. From the variation in size of the prints it was clear they were not made by hunters. There were children's footprints as well as a variety of adults'. He could only presume they were the Yuqui Indians.

Very little is known of the Yuqui Indians as they have only had brief and bloody encounters with the outside world. Once a priest went with his Bible to enlighten them. They shot a spear-sized arrow through his hand. They accomplished this amazing feat of accuracy with one of their huge, feet-drawn, bows. The priest did not heed the warning and was subsequently shot through the hip. He survived and now keeps the arrow on the wall of his Santa Cruz home.

The Yuquis have good reason to shoot on sight. The Bolivian military regularly exercised in Amboro, totally against the park authorities' wishes and used the Yuquis as target practice. This has only recently been stopped. Understandably therefore the Yuquis have kept their homes hidden and nobody knows exactly where they live.

Another tribe called the Yuracare have recently been contacted on the edge of the park. These people have been known to practice slavery and possibly cannibalism. They also have an interesting custom whereby when a tribe member dies they kill a relative, so that the dear-departed has a companion with whom to enter his after-life.

Most of these tribes quickly die out after the initial contact with the outside world. They catch diseases and find it impossible to adjust to our morality.

There was a recent case of a Yuracare man sentenced to life imprisonment. He was leaning against a wall in an outside village when a Camba Bolivian staggered up to him. The Camba was dead drunk and took a dislike to the Yuracare's strange appearance. He punched the Yuracare in the face. The Indian ran home, got his axe and chopped off the drunk's head. In his jungle morality, he had seen this unprovoked attack as a mortal offence and had reacted accordingly. He died a few months into his life sentence.

Unfortunately, people don't become any wiser, despite the horrendous failure rate of trying to Westernize these people. The priests still rush in with their Bibles and within the first few months of contact eighty per cent of the tribe die. Our ever-increasing desire for beefburgers pushes back the forests to expose these tribes to an incomprehensible world. People try to educate them as to the meaning of money and employment but they are forever being put in prison as they just borrow what they need from neighbours.

Anthropologists estimate that in 1500 the Amazon Basin had an Indian population of six to nine million. In 1900 there were one million Indians. Today there are less than 200,000. About half of the 230 tribes alive at the turn of the century, each with its own distinct culture, have been decimated and eighty-seven tribes have been exterminated.

I knew I was guilty of trespassing in the Yuqui's home but we had work to do. It was a sad indictment of society that the Yuqui's survival might rely on proving the existence of a turkey. If the forest was conserved to save a bird, the Yuquis might also live on.

After only two days in Buena Vista, Guy and I stocked up with food from the market, collected our clothes and headed back into the park. It was arranged that we meet Estaban in the park and that Clemente, who was on his patrol, would join us later. Guy and I walked uneventfully into the park and made it up to the study site. We pitched camp off the river in the general area where the hut was to be built. Estaban was not arriving for a couple of days, so we spent them searching for the curassow.

We climbed to the cliffs on the other side of the valley. Walking along the base we almost stumbled into a large stagnant pond. It was about thirty feet long, the water was totally black and therefore of indeterminate depth. We sat behind a tree, hoping to spot any thirsty wildlife. Nothing came along and strangely there were no tracks in the muddy banks. It seemed a perfect habitat for a large snake. I noticed no birds were singing and the only life was a couple of bright red dragonflies dive bombing each other. The eerie silence seemed to suggest some sinister presence. I could well imagine a huge anaconda lurking in the murky depths and I was happy when we moved off back along the cliffs.

After a further hour pushing our way through the undergrowth, we noticed a track heading up into the cliffs. Thinking it to be a tapir path, we followed it upwards. But branches and twigs on the trail were snapped at shoulder height. This was a human track!

Nobody else ever came this far into the jungle. Local hunters could catch all the animals they needed in the lower forest. Remembering Robin's warning, we guessed it might be the Yuquis. The thrill of unknown adventure made us follow the path. Our excitement increased as the path led up through the first cliffs and on towards a second ridge.

Weeks ago this path would have been quite invisible to me. Now, with heightened perceptions, it was as noticeable as a dual-carriageway. As we tracked onwards, looking for snapped twigs and worn depressions, I started to wonder what I would do if we stumbled upon the Yuquis. I was sure it would only happen if they wished it. In their element they would move silently, fading from tree to tree, shadow to shadow. I kept imagining myself with my hand held aloft, 'How! Me big white chief.' But I finally decided that I would more likely fall to the ground and quickly convert to religion.

We trekked on but as our adrenalin decreased we started to consider the ethics of what we were doing. We had no right to invade their home any more than was absolutely necessary. Also, daylight hours were running out, we had no water or provisions and so we decided to turn back. We were still greatly disappointed but we had no choice.

We set off back down the Yuqui path. It took us to the edge of a ten-foot-wide crevasse in the rocks, just below the cliffs. We decided this great gash in the ground would be a more interesting route back to camp and, watching my feet on the loose shingle, I slipped down the crevasse until thirty-foot walls of rock loomed over me. We searched for caves hoping to find a colony of oilbirds. They are so called because the Indians boil down the chicks to make cooking and light oil. We had heard an oilbird screeching over the camp a few nights before and we wanted to verify the existence of these rare cave-dwellers. Oilbirds are nocturnal and they have a simple radar system emitting as many as 250 clicks a second which helps them to navigate in the dark. It is not as sophisticated as a bat's radar but they can still pilot a night flight through the trees.

Unfortunately we were unsuccessful in our search but only a few steps out of the other end of the crevasse, Guy, walking slightly ahead, disturbed two large birds and they flew up into a tree. He pointed out their silhouettes against the rapidly approaching dusk. By the time I had located a large black body and white-tipped tail, the birds had glided off down into the valley. Guy had seen them distinctly before they flew off. They were horned curassows. I had caught only a fleeting glimpse but it boded well for the future.

We made it back to camp just before the shadows merged into blackness. It had been a close thing. It is difficult enough to navigate in the daylight but in the dark it would have been impossible. We could have passed within ten feet of the camp and never have known. Wandering around the jungle at night is almost suicidal.

Grateful to have reached camp, we sat talking about the day. The decision to turn back had been made for us but we still felt tempted to follow the path. It might lead to hidden Inca temples, abandoned cities, gold.

The dilemma was that there was a great deal of work to do, collecting data on the curassow but the urge to explore into the heart of the park was almost irresistible. The problem was time. Within a month the wet season might start and entry into the park would become impossible. The only way in was by the rivers and these would become raging torrents only hours, possibly minutes, after the first heavy rains. A storm could strike at any moment and last for weeks, cutting us off from the outside and stranding us at the top of a hill surrounded by raging rapids. Also if there were rains in the centre of the park then flash floods could strike with amazing speed and force. The rivers would carry tonnes of rock as easily as pebbles. These flash floods are rather understatedly called 'freshets'. The word seemed too genteel to describe killer rapids.

If we were going to follow the path, we would have to plan carefully. We decided to concentrate on building the house. With it built, we would have more protection from potentially deadly weather changes and perhaps then we could launch a major expedition to follow the path to wherever it led.

Early next morning Estaban arrived. He was bigger than Clemente and had also been a hunter. He had a large watch and a packet of cigarettes stuck out of the top pocket of his park shirt which he wore with pride. He shook my hand shyly and then quickly set to work, surveying the camp area for the best place to build the house, conscious of floods even on this elevated site.

Estaban continually grew in my estimation. He did

everything with such mindless expertise. For example we would try for ages to light a fire. Scrunching up paper under carefully selected kindling, we would complete the idyllic boy scout camp fire with an artistic teepee of small branches. Just to make sure of success we would soak it in a squirt of medicinal neat alcohol. It would flare up and within seconds die out. Estaban would smile to himself and pick up a few leaves. He would light them with his cigarette lighter, heave a huge log on to the flickering pile and within minutes we would have a roaring fire.

Estaban had brought with him an axe head. He built up the fire and stuck the axe head in the heart of the flames to burn out the old handle. He then walked around the camp, eyeing up the trees and stroking their branches, in deep contemplation. He eventually selected a particular bough and with a few accurate machete blows he severed it and sat down cross-legged by the fire with the branch wedged between his feet. He then honed it with the long, clumsy machete. After twenty minutes he'd slotted his axe head over the handle. The surface was so smooth it could have been turned on a lathe and then varnished.

We marked out and started to clear the building area. The only tools available were a hoe, two machetes and an axe but with a few days' effort we managed to clear and level the site. We then dug holes for the supporting posts. With the hoe we had to dig a vertical shaft a metre deep. If it was going to be any use to create sound foundations, the hole would have to be as narrow as possible.

The first hole was dug without too much difficulty. The second proved a little more awkward as several small rocks blocked our progress. With each hole, it became increasingly clear that we had pinpointed with surprising accuracy the only underground jungle quarry. A metre doesn't seem very deep but when digging with nothing but a hoe into almost solid rock, it becomes a trifle difficult. We took it in turns to cut away at the solid earth. Guy's hands and mine steadily became blistered and bloody.

Estaban, however, was working consistently without the slightest sign of abrasions. He looked at our hands and, smiling at his own superiority, led us over to the little fire he always kept smouldering day and night, beckoning for us to hold our hands in the smoke. This was apparently his secret remedy. He would regularly hold his hands in the smoke. I'm not sure whether it toughened them or made them more malleable, but we suffered no more blisters with regular treatment.

The ninth and final hole had the tip of a mountain one foot under the surface. We widened our hole hoping to find the edge and prise it out. When the hole was almost five feet across, we gave up and decided to chip away at the boulder until we had a reasonably satisfactory depth. Toiling away with the hoe for an hour would only get us down a few centimetres. Even the axe only made slight splinters fly off the rock. We spent an entire day on this one hole.

With this continual exertion I was introduced to another Amazonian insect. These were small black bees called sweat bees. I would be constantly hounded by them and, while resting, well over a hundred would swarm around me landing on my body to lick up the salt. They don't bite or sting but with so many around, they fly into your eyes and mouth, up your nose and buzz loudly in your ears. I hated them with such passion that whenever they flew into my mouth, I would gnash them up with my teeth before spitting them out.

Just as we finished the final hole Clemente miraculously arrived. He also wore his park guard shirt with pride and automatically took charge of the situation, his status emphasized by owning the one and only official park gun. He carried this imported survivor of the First World War slung over his shoulder. It looked dangerously like a musket and was almost the same height as he was.

Any admiration for Estaban's jungle craft was premature as Clemente proceeded to make it look infantile.

Before he started work on our house, he built his own shelter. Within minutes he had built a bunkbed bungalow. He allowed himself the luxury of using one unnatural material. His sloping roof was guaranteed waterproof by lining it with plastic sheeting. I watched a craftsman in action: his careful selection of branches, the very few strokes he needed to cut his materials. He demonstrated to me how he made the palm rope he used to bind it all together, the size and type of palm that made the best rope and how it was unnecessary to chop down the tree. He did all of this in under an hour although he seemed almost to be working in slow motion. His top bunk where he would sleep was five feet and his bottom bunk two feet off the ground. He used this to dry and store firewood and to store his food.

Estaban, feeling a little outshone, set about building his own shelter. Within a couple of hours there was a rather ostentatious, double-bunkbed house standing beside Clemente's sensible one-up-one-down.

We worked all week, Guy and I doing the more manual labour. We carried the cut trees and palms back to the house site. Clemente was generally in charge of the axe and despite his diminutive stature, he wielded it with power and incredible precision. His musical voice echoed his comments and suggestions through the jungle. Always with a broad grin on his face, a green bobble hat on his head and cheeks puffed out, his mouth crammed with coca leaves, he was the perfect foreman.

We made steady progress but unfortunately Clemente started to feel unwell. When we were not looking he would curl up by the fire and his little body would shudder as a coughing fit swept through him. When he noticed we were watching, he would jump to his feet and pretend he was fine. For a couple of days there was no improvement and he was shivering almost constantly so Guy sent him home. Apparently he had been ill for over a year with tuberculosis. He would not spend any of his savings on medicines for himself and kept his money in case his children fell ill. He was also unprepared to risk time off work, as he thought he might lose his job. If he lost his job, his family would starve.

I was caught in a dilemma of whether to go with him or to go on my own, five days later. I had to renew my visa down in Santa Cruz as I had been given only a month's tourist visa on entry. If I went with him, I would be a week early in Buena Vista.

Despite everyone's warnings about doing things in pairs, I decided to walk out alone. With the continual race against the wet season, Guy would have to stay and continue building the house. I was not so scared of the animals, more of getting lost. Clemente promised to mark the path more clearly for me on his way out. I made my preparations so that I could leave early in the morning and I set off as soon as it was light, just before six. After four hours I left the river and I was walking so quietly that I chanced upon some wildlife.

On the path ahead of me was a great crashing of branches and then two roars finishing in a sort of bark. In the darkness of the jungle floor I caught sight of a large shape and as it disappeared into the shadows, I recognized a dog-like tail. I froze, desperately trying to remain in control of my bowels. My body had taken on strange jelly-like qualities. Even my skeleton was wobbling. Deciding noise and bravado were my best tactics, I picked up a large stick and as the only way was forward I strode boldly in an attempt to fool my fear. I took a couple of practice swings with the stick as I approached the brute's last known position and smacked my weapon against a tree trunk. It disintegrated, leaving nothing but a rotten stump in my hand. Standing defenceless in the heart of the beast's lair, my eyes implored the ground, desperate for a new weapon.

Expecting to have my throat ripped out at any second, I noticed the trees crowding round me. In seconds I became an expert on ambush techniques, as I logically worked out from where the attack would come. I spotted another branch and snatched it up. Feeling its solidity in my hand, my battle mode forced me to whisper boldly, 'Try me!'

The jungle became deathly quiet as if in silent derision of my pathetic challenge. I walked uncertainly forward through the dark shadows in slow motion readying my stick for each expected attack. Nothing came and as I strode on my hair felt electrically charged. Breaking through into a clearing, I let out the shudder that had been simmering in my taut muscles.

I was unable to throw down the cumbersome stick for hours, even though I was fortunately free of gushing bite wounds.

Later when I described the experience to Robin he replied excitedly that it must have been the extremely rare bush dog.

'Not rare enough,' I mused.

As I walked on my miseries increased. It started to thunder, the rain pelting my face. Every time I believed it wouldn't get harder, nature would prove me wrong. But it wasn't the discomfort that really worried me. I imagined the river paths to be disappearing with every step. I lengthened my stride, forgetting all fatigue, bush dogs and rain, fearing the worst possible end: lost in the Amazon rainforest.

Fortunately when I left the jungle and rejoined one of the rivers the rain had actually made tracking easier. The slight depression made by our feet had filled with water, marking an obvious stream only a foot wide. This part of the journey crossed rivers forcing me to re-enter the jungle and then cross back on to the wide sand banks of another river. There were no recognizable landmarks and all the sand banks looked the same. I had been particularly worried about this stretch and so I was mightily relieved to see the rain had helped mark my path. With forced speed I made Terminal by three o'clock. I had only stopped three times for a brief cigarette in nine hours' marching.

Reaching Terminal there was no sign of life until a woman came out of her hut to look at me. She said something and I guessed she was asking where I was going. I said Buena Vista. She shook her head indicating that I would never get a lift that day. I was still twenty kilometres from my sofa so I set off again.

I had walked about five kilometres when a youth ran out of his house and asked where I was going. He shook his head and said Buena Vista was a very long way away. But for seven bolivianos he would take me on the back of his motor-bike. With the obsessive determination it had taken to come this far, I wasn't about to let a native boy get the better of me. I told him I'd pay five bolivianos. He replied he had to ask for seven as the petrol was very expensive for such a long journey. I shook my head and walked on.

He broke, shouting after me that he would do it for five. I grinned insanely and pulled out my bundle of notes selecting a five. This crazy bartering had saved me fifty pence in real terms. I believe such was my sun-addled resolve I would have walked on rather than lose.

He drove me, helmetless, on his little motor-bike to Buena Vista, weaving in and out of the potholes and stray cattle.

*

CHAPTER 8

Tapir

I arrived back in Buena Vista and called on Robin. I arranged to go down to Santa Cruz the next day with Miriam, his Bolivian wife, who had a relative working in immigration who could speed up the formalities.

The trip down was quite eventful as the recent rains had washed away some of the foundations of a wooden bridge. There was a soldier stationed to make sure that passengers disembarked from their buses and walked across, while the driver said a short prayer, shut his eyes and hoped for the best. The bridge groaned but managed to stay upright. We repacked ourselves among the chickens and rice bags and drove on to Santa Cruz.

Miriam's brother-in-law said he could get me a year visa for one hundred and thirty dollars. Off my guard I paid him and said I would return later. When I did he said unfortunately he had only managed to get me a three-month visa, which also cost one hundred and thirty dollars. I had no receipt so there was no arguing but I cursed myself to be on guard against the ever-present corruption.

I returned directly to Buena Vista to find Guy had come out of the park. The rain stopped the work and they needed materials and help to continue the job. Valerie had also returned and had bought provisions. It was arranged that Valerie and I would go back into the park the next morning and Guy and Robin would follow in a few days' time.

We set off early, Valerie setting a good pace. We never considered splitting the weight of our supplies unevenly. Valerie carried her share and it was never questioned she would do otherwise. I was quite happy to let her lead. I used her wiggly bottom as a carrot to coax me forward. Hour after hour it would entice me onward, helping me to forget fatigue.

We reached the midway hut uneventfully and went to cool off in the otter pool. We called it the otter pool because an otter lived there, although no one except Valerie had ever seen it. Floating in the pool, Valerie turned towards me, 'If you could have anything you wanted right now what would it be?'

I considered this at length as a small catfish nibbled the tick bite scars on my legs.

'I'd like to be stretched out on a large cumfy sofa with a Norwegian nymphet, watching the Christmas special of *Only Fools and Horses*. What would you like?'

She replied without hesitation, 'A plate of roast beef and Yorkshire pudding.'

'With cauliflower cheese?'

'Yes, and loads of roast potatoes.'

'And carrots and thick gravy?'

'And English mustard.'

'And a big bottle of red wine?'

'And then rhubarb crumble . . . and custard.'

'Ahh, you're so right! Sod the nymphet, I'd like the roast beef as well.'

'Yeah, yummeee!'

'Mmmm.'

We spent an increasing amount of time fantasizing about food. It was not surprising, the only two forms of protein available being sardines and spam.

I swatted away the catfish and asked, 'What are we going to eat tonight? Not sardines and rice again!'

'No, tonight as a special treat we are going to have rice and sardines instead.'

'Valerie, you know the saying – the way to a man's heart is through his stomach?'

'Yes.'

'Well, from the extensive menu you have dreamed up, I can only presume you hate me very, very much.'

'Yes.'

That evening I was upset to discover how similar rice and sardines tasted compared with sardines and rice.

We set off at nine the next morning to walk up to the study site. We came out of the oppressive jungle on to the river with the usual sense of relief. After a few kilometres we sat down at a small spring for a rest. Reclining luxuriantly on a rock I surveyed the fantastic scenery. I noticed large ripples in a deep pool thirty metres up stream. Two ears popped up, swivelling and twitching like a sound periscope. They were followed by a brown mane of erect bristle hair. It was not until it stuck its trunk out to suck in air that I recognized it as a tapir. A tapir is the largest jungle mammal. It is the size of a large pig with half an elephant trunk. Unfortunately tapirs are now rare as their meat is a greatly prized delicacy.

I pointed excitedly, 'Tapir!'

The tapir decided to immerse itself completely, so Valerie, following my arm, could see nothing. She looked at me annoyed that I was fooling around.

'No, really, there's a tapir, look!'

It was now paddling only half-submerged and it sploshed about, quite oblivious of us, for some minutes. It then stepped out of the pool, shook itself in a doglike fashion and ambled down the opposite river bank towards us. Flies swarmed around its head as it sauntered along. We remained motionless, confident that it must soon detect us and bolt for the cover of the jungle.

Tapirs are generally nocturnal animals, relying more on smell than eyesight. But during the heat of the day they are known to bathe for long periods. We had caught him having a late-morning dip.

Even if we stayed still it must surely smell us soon. But we were either down wind or it had a cold, because it continued to trot steadily towards us. At twenty feet it began to cross the water separating us. It was coming to find out what we were. It stopped six feet away and sniffed, wrinkling its long nose. It lowered its trunk to drink a little water, perhaps to clear its confused sinuses. It had never smelled human before and therefore didn't know to fear us. It was a great compliment to the success of the park.

However, I was wondering if tapirs could catch rabies. Maybe this was a mad, killer, rabies-ridden tapir? My hand curled round my Swiss army penknife, readying for action. I selected the saw blade as it was the easiest to flick out. The tapir turned its head side on to us, so that one eye could study us in detail. It rolled the eye in slow deliberate movement so that all sides of white were exposed. Convinced that it could neither eat nor mate with us, it gave one last disappointed sniff and waddled back across the river, along the bank and up into the jungle.

We had sat motionless for the entire five-minute period. It took another couple of minutes before we could speak.

'I thought it was going to go for us!'

'I had my penknife ready.'

In the elation of having come within feet of a large wild animal that was without fear, we made good progress to base camp. We pitched tent next to the building site.

The next evening, after an entire day's unsuccessful curassow stalking, we returned to camp. I was sitting in the firelight, reading and trying to put names to the birds I had seen. Valerie was putting the supper on. She asked me where I had hidden the rice. Without looking up, I gestured vaguely in the direction of the pile of food.

'Yes, well, I can't find it!'

I moaned, unaware that her interruption would save my life. I put down the book and made to push myself up to help find it.

I froze, my arms locked, holding my bottom off the ground. No more than two feet away, and approaching fast, was a large red, yellow and black banded snake. All those years of watching American television cop shows paid dividends. I did my best Starsky and Hutch roll to get out of its path.

It bunched itself up and struck at my departing rump. I expect this was a purely reflex strike, as its fangs missed me by at least an inch.

Valerie looked at me as if I were mad and then spotted the snake. I was strangely breathless until I realized that it was because I wasn't breathing. I sucked in air, savouring the taste of every gas it contains.

The snake had coiled itself up into a ball ready to strike and was hissing aggressively. My first reaction had been, it's a coral snake. The jungle rhyme 'Red and yellow can kill a fellow!' had played in my mind in the brief frozen moment in which I had relived most of my life. It was a sad realization that I could fit it all in.

Many snakes have a territory they rarely move from. If our house was in this snake's territory we would never be able to sleep safely as it would hunt out our body warmth.

Robin had also been telling me the only way positively to identify species of reptiles was to supply the Santa Cruz University with specimens. We agreed we should kill it. As the only resident expert, I was nominated for the task. Valerie, bravely standing behind me, handed me the two-foot-long iron bar we used to hold our cooking pots in the fire. I tried to hand it back.

I had read books about reptile collecting and the recommended way of killing a snake without damaging its carcass is to inject it with cyanide. But the one time you need your syringe dart full of cyanide you can be almost positive you will have left it on the kitchen table with the elephant gun. This time was no exception. I had to settle for the iron bar.

The next best recommended way is to hit the snake on the heart. All I could think of was, who writes these books? I also felt particularly bitter towards my mother, who in

not letting me keep snakes, had denied me my usual practice of dissecting all deceased pets. I usually did this on
the kitchen table with the magnanimous consideration of
laying down newspaper first. However, I had a vague idea
that the heart would be five or six inches from the base of
its head. I edged forward, trying to position myself to
clobber the snake. The snake was equally intent on giving
me a poisoned kiss.

It struck out, its mouth agape and fangs eager to stab.
I could see down its pink throat as I leapt out of range.
Its unsuccessful lunge had momentarily stretched it out
over the rock I had been sitting on. Before it could recoil
I whacked down with the bar scoring a direct hit. We
stood back and watched as it writhed into death.

The whole incident had not lasted more than a minute.
As it slowly died, twisting and pointlessly fighting for life,
blood trickling from the wound, my adrenalin stopped
pumping and I was filled with horrified remorse.

I knew in that moment that my brief herpetological
career was over. There was no way I could run around the
countryside clubbing things to death. Collecting specimens may be a necessary part of the job but I wasn't going
to do it. The prospect of jars full of specimens had appealed
while back in England but now it held no recom-
mendations.

As I stood watching the snake die, I was able to study
it. It struck me that it was far too long to be a coral snake.
I knew of a harmless snake called a 'false coral snake',
which is so named because it looks like a coral snake except
that it is longer. This snake was four feet long while a
proper coral does not grow longer than a metre. This made
me feel even worse as I picked it up rather carelessly. Even
with a dead snake, extreme care must be taken when
picking it up. A snake can retain the reflex strike action
for up to a day after it has died. A dead snake could
therefore wreak revenge from the grave twenty-four hours
after you killed it.

In death its fangs seemed almost non-existent. However, it was now dead and so I was not going to waste this sacrifice. I pickled it in a powdered milk tin with our medicinal alcohol. It now resides in a jar in Santa Cruz natural history museum with my name as collector pinned to it. It is displayed because it proved to be the extremely rare and the most poisonous snake in South America, *Micrurus spixi*, or giant coral snake. They are said by the experts not to be aggressive and that they only bite when handled or stood on. Unfortunately the experts had forgotten to tell my snake that. The only advantage of being bitten by a coral snake is that its poison acts like an anaesthetic. You painlessly drift off to sleep and never wake up.

Guy and Robin arrived the next morning and were very impressed with the snake, which we had christened Herbert. No further progress could be made on the house until Robin had organized the hiring of a few local builders. Estaban and Clemente needed help with the skilful task of crafting the roof and walls. We therefore spent the next few days in pairs searching for the curassow.

My ears gradually became tuned to the curassow call but it had taken a great deal of patience. Once I had learnt to distinguish its call I couldn't understand why I hadn't been able to hear it before. Without knowing it I was becoming attuned to the jungle as a whole. It's like an innate survival wisdom. You don't notice your change of behaviour, it becomes a natural sixth sense. You automatically check where you put your hands and feet. You rarely touch anything, if possible avoiding all contact. The reason is the proximity of poisonous animals and insects, also many of the plants are viciously protected with barbs and thorns. Clearly, to survive in such a hostile environment you had to adapt.

The call of the curassow is a very deep resonant 'ummmm'. Only very deep or very high-pitched sounds can travel for any distance through the dense jungle. I now heard the noise regularly, but the elusive bird would stop calling when we got within a few hundred metres.

The next day Guy and I spent over an hour creeping within two hundred metres of the noise. We were rewarded when we disturbed two large birds. One flew off down the valley but the other sought sanctity in a tree. I recognized it from the description I'd been given, as it stood clearly silhouetted against the sky. It was a large handsome bird but its horn was totally remarkable: it was bright blue. It stuck out of its forehead, as noticeable as a police beacon and about the size of a large thumb. It seemed almost to glow. This was the unicorn!

Casup! Casup! Casup! It perched nervously in the tree, shrieking its loud warning call. Guy busily snapped away with his camera but the bird took off to glide down into the valley. I had seen it for no more than twenty seconds but as there are fewer than ten non-Indians who have ever seen it, this was no mean achievement. The Indians' local name for it is *copete piedra azul* which roughly translates as blue rockhead. The Indians had a talent for names.

Guy and I saw the same two birds the next day. Valerie and Robin also saw a curassow but used another technqiue of approaching without causing fear. They pretended to be a herd of wild pigs, crashing through the jungle making snorting noises. I preferred the softly softly approach and so was a little apprehensive when Robin suggested the two of us spend the following day searching further up the valley. That evening I practised my snorts and grunts but fortunately Robin believed one day pretending to be a pig was enough. He led me silently through the forest, identifying birds and animal tracks. His trained eyes spotted much that I missed and high up in a tree he pointed out a large blue and yellow macaw. His enthusiasm was infectious and his knowledge astounding.

On the way back to camp we rested on the boulders of a little stream. The last rays of the afternoon sun heated the rocks and illuminated a young sapling that stood alone on a raised island platform. As we sat chatting, a fine spray jetted out of the tree, creating a rainbow around us. A few seconds later another jet spurted out. We climbed up to study the tiny tree. We could see no hole and the tree didn't oblige us with another squirt. We couldn't understand whether it was some buried insect or a result of osmosis. We christened the intriguing phenomenon 'The Pissing Tree'. We left it unresolved and walked back to camp.

I was now considered initiated to the curassow and familiar with its call and it was decided to do a provisional population survey. The study area, although no larger than a few square kilometres, encompassed three types of habitat. There was high clear forest with large trees and very little undergrowth, low forest with slightly fewer big trees and finally there was the virtually impentrable thickets along the small river tributaries. The curassows had been seen in all these places.

We needed more pens, paper and another wristwatch to start the surveys so we decided to leave the next day.

That evening, as it drizzled with rain, I went to fetch some water. We collected our water from a little stream. The only animals that might pollute it were the tapirs. They had an unsual and unpleasant habit of defecating in the rivers and pools, especially at the tops of hills. I sat filling the container with water, trying not to disturb the murk on the bottom of the steam.

There was movement under the bank. The water was dark and with no direct sunlight I couldn't see anything in the shadows. Another ripple and I caught sight of it. It was a newt. I grabbed for it but missed. It disappeared into the grimy depths. I sat and waited but it didn't reappear.

Although I was no expert, I hadn't known there were newts in South America. I asked everyone to keep an eye out for it.

CHAPTER 9

*

Anita

Guy and I went to Santa Cruz to develop the curassow photos and buy supplies. The photos were a disappointment. Only three out of twelve taken showed the all-important horn and even these were blurred and dark.

Guy took me to the university to meet Paolo. Paolo worked in the biology department and almost single-handed he had created a natural history museum on the university campus. He had mounted and identified all the exhibits and also caught many of them. He was very excited with my account of the newt. He said he knew of only two species of newt in South America and that in such unexplored areas new species were a very real possibility. He asked me to make every attempt to catch it.

Guy and I returned to Buena Vista and walking from the plaza we met Charo. She was carrying a baby and I was rather surprised when she introduced me to her daughter. This slender and beautiful young girl I'd first met in the Amboro office and estimated was fourteen, was in fact nineteen and a parent. I'd noticed many young girls had babies but apparently no one had sex. Even from my limited knowledge gleaned from a red-faced biology teacher I knew the two to be related. I decided to put in some research and get to the bottom of this puzzle. I asked Charo if she had a sister. She had and she would be at the graduation dance that night. We were cordially invited.

The whole town was there to celebrate the students' school graduation. The party was held in an open yard off the plaza. Fortunately the evening was clear and warm.

The locals had gone to great efforts to dress smartly. Most people had very little money but their appearance did not suffer.

The mayor had hired a four-piece traditional band from Santa Cruz and they set up their instruments on the brick stage. Guy, Valerie and I were the only gringos there. We were therefore the subject of much conversation and pointing.

Despite the band knowing only three chords, the locals packed on to the unevenly paved dance floor. I watched, trying to pick up the subtleties of the dance step. There were none. They all danced in couples but they never touched or looked at each other. It was therefore difficult to identify a particular couple to study. The dance was more monotonous than the music. After much analysis I picked up the basics. They took a couple of shuffles forward and then a couple of shuffles back. The object seemed to be to move as little as possible and to avoid all physical and eye contact with your partner.

Valerie and I decided to have a go. Much to the amusement of the locals, we shuffled back and forth, looking blankly at the ground or up at the sky. We couldn't keep it up. This lack of movement was clearly going to take a lot of practice. We strutted off to get some beer.

They kept the bottles in a large, water-filled trough. The barman pulled out two bottles and, using a half-exposed nail in the wall, he de-capped them. The music had stopped and a man on the stage was speaking into a microphone cunningly wired to a car battery. It was time for the graduation ceremony. The locals formed a human corridor for the graduates to walk down. Everyone clapped as this year's successful school leavers were led down the aisle. There were about seven and they were each accompanied by their mother or father. After a short speech from the mayor, everyone clapped and got on with the shuffle dancing.

Valerie and Guy decided to leave and so we went to say

goodbye to Charo and her friends. As we stood chatting, my eyes were captured by a vision of womanhood. A young beauty sat hand in hand with her boyfriend. She crossed her elegant legs beneath a short black lace skirt. She looked up, her large brown eyes holding me in a challenging stare. I smiled and she smiled back with an impish confidence that suggested a wickedly mischievous character.

She lifted her boyfriend's hand from the neutral space between them and rested it with her own on her delicate knee. My eyes followed the gesture and after a few detours they worked their way back to her face. Confident she had my complete attention she asked, 'Would you like to dance?'

I laughed but she showed no humour. Realizing she was serious I searched her eyes for a motive. She stared back, confident of my reply.

I looked back down at her knee and her hand still coupled with the boyfriend's. This time I followed his arm up to his face. He looked away, pretending indifference. However, his jaw hinted at hostility. She was playing games with us both.

'No, thank you,' I replied and in my pidgin Spanish I explained I considered it bad form to ask strangers to dance, especially when you're out with a boyfriend.

Her smile had wavered and so I added, 'I don't even know your name.'

She paused before smiling provocatively, 'I'm Anita, Charo's sister.'

'Maybe another time, Anita.'

'Yes,' my ego heard promises. I had no doubt I would be grappling with her fastenings pretty damn soon.

I marked Anita down for definite further investigation. I said goodnight and shook her boyfriend's hand. I left her with another direct smile which she met unflinchingly. The challenge had been set and the gauntlet taken. But she'd have to work hard. I wasn't going to be easy.

I had to put romance on hold because the next day we

went back into the jungle. It took Guy and I two hours longer than normal to walk to Clemente's hut. We hoped to do all three area surveys in this one visit and therefore needed supplies for up to three weeks. The guards would willingly have hunted for us but no hunting was the basic principle of the park. We were carrying over thirty kilograms of sardines, spam, vegetables and rice each. Some of the supplies were left for Clemente and Estaban to bring up.

When we arrived at the study site in the early afternoon of the next day the house was still a skeleton so we pitched the tent. We spent the afternoon cutting a path with machetes to the first survey area. This set of hides was close to where we had found the Yuqui Indian path but although we searched thoroughly we found no sign of it. We never discovered it again. This spooked me as I guessed that the Yuquis, realizing our presence, had deliberately hidden their tracks.

Valerie and Estaban arrived the next day. Estaban delivered some supplies and then left as he had to prepare to bring in the local builders.

It thundered for two days and nights and our waterproof tents were washed out. We sought refuge under Clemente's food-storage table. We covered it in plastic sheeting and lived under it for forty-eight hours, eating only cold sardines. Hundreds of frogs and toads sploshed around in the puddles. They sat in front of our table, snapping up the moths our candles attracted. An explosion of brightly coloured poison arrow frogs hopped everywhere but the queen of all the amphibians made her presence felt. A nine-inch giant toad wobbbled round the camp like an ancient punctured leather football. She would squat and glare with stony eyes as we ate our evening meal. Lacking inspration, we called her Toad. She spent most evenings with us, eating anything that came within reach of her cavernous mouth.

The next day the rain stopped and Clemente arrived.

We built the first set of hides and sent Clemente off to
start the next set. When we'd finished we went to see how
he'd got on. He had attacked the problem with his usual
enthusiasm, constructing a prototype copied from an Ideal
Home exhibition. We told him it was very nice but could
the other two be a little smaller. After a couple more days'
work we were ready to start our survey. Clemente left to
collect building supplies for the house.

We were in our respective hides for six the next
morning. The hides were the three corners of a north,
south and east triangle. They were approximately one
hundred and fifty metres apart, as this was the estimated
maximum carrying distance of the curassow call. We
hoped our results would therefore only duplicate calls
made between the hides. In principle this would maximize
the area we could survey.

Around each hide we placed eight stakes showing the
main compass points. The curassow call was about six
notes, of conveniently different volumes. Therefore the
number of notes heard would give a fair indication of its
distance from the hide. For each call we would log:
distance, position and exact time. Six hours doing this
every morning was immeasurably boring. I filled in time
by shaving with the scissors in my penknife. The tiny
blades could only cut a whisker with each snip so this
would keep me occupied for about three hours. The rest
of the time I carved wooden ornaments, made up crosswords and killed insects.

The afternoons would be spent washing, collecting
water and searching for firewood. Valerie had taught herself how to make bread in the saucepan over the campfire.
For a special treat we would make tea with real powdered
milk and have it with toast and jam. Very occasionally
a troop of spider monkeys would visit. Sipping our tea we
would watch as they threw themselves from branch to
branch with astounding agility. They chased each other
along the boughs in a never-ending contest of skill and

bravery. But as quickly as they arrived they would disappear, screeching and howling down into the valley.

In the evenings we would cook our one and only meal of the day. Everyone's favourite was another Valerie creation, spam and onion rissoles. She battered the spam burgers with a pancake mix and fried them. By the time we had cooked the food it would be dark so it was quite common to have an unexpected mouthful of moth with the rissoles. If they were too big to crunch we'd throw them towards Toad. She wasn't so fussy and gratefully gobbled them up.

We would do each other's crosswords and we even had a go at campfire singing. We didn't get much mileage from the entertainment, however, as the only song all three of us knew was 'Gordon is a Moron'. Mostly we would talk about food and listen to the jungle noises. Owls hooted and distant tapirs would let out shrill whistles. The most prevalent noise was the ear-splitting whine of the elusive cicada insect. I heard them all around me but I never saw one. If the moon was up we might catch a glimpse of a night monkey's silhouette as it crashed through the trees.

As we sat in the firelight, vampire bats swooped around us. The vampire bats I'd seen in London Zoo had been tiny things but our nocturnal visitors were more like crows. They hoped we would fall asleep so they could tap us for a quick half pint. We would go to bed as soon as we felt tired as they were potential carriers of rabies and therefore a considerable danger.

We moved on to the second set of hides and Valerie announced she had two borros. After a lot of rain a borro fly lays its eggs, sometimes on clothes. These eggs hatch and the tiny maggot digs down a hair follicle. Once under your skin it springs out bristles to anchor it firmly and then sends up a tube so it can breathe. Then for about three weeks it lives under your skin, eating away at your flesh. When it's about an inch long, it digs out, falls to the ground and pupates.

Valerie had two, one in her leg and the other in her scalp. Guy had had one in his hip the last trip but I'd yet to experience this delightful creature. The tropical medicine book recommended you block its airhole with Airfix glue. While packing in England, by some bizarre lack of foresight, I hadn't considered Airfix glue. Instead we tried to suffocate them using vaseline. With a considerable amount of patience we managed to grab them as they came up for air and yank them out.

The guards arrived the next day with three local builders. They set to work chopping down palm trees. They split the trunks to build walls and used the leaves to thatch the roof. The results from the third set of hides were spoilt as the curassows were scared by the banging, chopping and hammering.

Valerie and I sat one afternoon watching the builders work. They seemed oblivious to the swarms of sweat bees. We overheard Clemente and Estaban chatting. They were discussing what they would do if they were very rich.

'I would sing and dance all day!'

Estaban nodded his solemn agreement. It seemed an ideal worth striving for.

I walked off, not wishing to intrude, when I heard something crashing through the forest below camp. Investigating, I spotted a family group of opossums. These South American marsupials look like large grey rats. They made a tremendous noise as they foraged for bugs. When they finally ran off I headed back to camp and told Clemente. He looked very disappointed that he had missed them.

'They make good eating,' he told me. 'Not that I hunt them anymore,' he added quickly, realizing his blunder.

The builders finished the house and left. Our supplies were running out so we only stayed one night in the completed house. We had arranged with Robin which day we could come out and so he borrowed a Land Rover and came to pick us up. He risked the four-wheel-drive vehicle against the Surutu river and was able to come all the way to Arnaldo's farm. After twenty days in the jungle, a car was a tremendous culture shock.

Hearing the Land Rover approaching I had to control an incredibly strong urge to run back into the forest. Fighting down the irrational panic, I realized I wouldn't have to walk any further. I was calm enough to look at myself in the wing mirror – not bad, although I needed a haircut.

*

CHAPTER 10

Something for the
Weekend, Sir?

After such a long time away from civilization I was desperate for news of home so Valerie and I went to Santa Cruz to pick up the mail. I was particularly sad to read that the geraniums in the hanging baskets had finished flowering.

We had lunch in one of the European bars. I was to go there often when I was down in Santa Cruz and I got to know a few of the patrons. They were mainly English and German men in their forties and fifties. Most were washed-out alcoholics who worked in the twilight business – cocaine. They weren't the big boys, they were just packers and transporters. I saw so much of myself in their characters. They had left their home countries as young men with high ideals and the lust for adventure. For a few years their youth and exuberance had knocked down all obstacles. But the continual rigours of life on the road had worn them down. Drawn to Bolivia like vultures by the new cocaine prosperity, they found no pot of gold, just more impossible dreams. Unable to leave, they had sunk to packing cocaine in cameras, wooden carvings and cattle carcasses. They were now husks of men who bickered over pennies.

We left them to their half bottles of neat alcohol and set off to find a hairdresser's. Valerie had decided she also wanted her hair cutting so we went to a small unisex shop a few streets from the central plaza.

As usual in a male-dominated society I would have

my hair cut first while Valerie waited. I felt increasingly uncomfortable at the amount of time the barber was spending on my hair. The shop was filling up with young women who just sat patiently chatting and reading magazines. I noticed a particularly attractive peroxide-blonde girl and I nearly lost an ear trying to smile at her. A large woman started to cut Valerie's hair. She asked Valerie, 'Are you his woman?'

Valerie replied, 'I certainly am not.'

The female barber joked, 'Can I be, then?'

Everyone laughed heartily. I sat confused at this merriment of which I was clearly the butt. I was unable to keep up with all the Spanish so I asked Valerie to translate.

'She said you have a gorgeous bottom and she wants to sleep with you.'

'Umm, gosh. Tell her that would be very nice but unfortunately I haven't had my vitamins today.'

'He says you are very beautiful,' Valerie relayed back to the hairdresser.

The girls giggled and smiled at me provocatively. I reciprocated rather nervously as the lady hairdresser looked distinctly powerful. She seemed surprisingly pleased with my gentle rebuff.

I had become used to this female attention. Being a gringo made you instantly eligible, whatever your appearance.

After the barber had finished I asked if they had a toilet. He pointed down a corridor at the back of the shop. On my way back I noticed some curtained cubicles with what appeared to be doctors' couches inside. In the third cubicle the curtain was pulled back and I heard a voice from within. I glimpsed in without breaking stride. Inside, reclining on a bench, was the blonde with her legs unfortunately positioned so I could see up her skirt.

'Come in and play,' she purred.

'I'm sorry, I don't understand Spanish,' was my standard reply.

I walked on a few more steps wondering what she had said to me. Before I could make a decision to turn back to see if I could decipher it, I was greeted by the barber. Slightly disappointed, I went and sat at the front of the shop.

Valerie decided to have her hair tinted so she would be quite a while. The male barber didn't start to cut the hair of any of the young girls, so I presumed they were either other hairdressers or family. The barber offered me a Coca-Cola and a more comfortable seat in the rear of the shop in front of the back corridor. From on top of the fridge he offered me a magazine. The other hairdressers lounged around me waiting for the afternoon rush. He handed me the magazine with the comment *'por hombres'*. It was hard porn and I felt extremely uncomfortable reading it while surrounded by young women. I didn't want to snub the barber so I perused it as briefly as possible. Ten minutes later, my duty satisfied, I put the literature down on the table.

The barber asked Valerie if I would like a nail manicure.

'How much does it cost?' I enquired.

She translated the question.

'Two bolivianos.'

'It's free,' Valerie informed.

'OK,' I nodded dumbly.

One of the young girls pulled her chair up to sit in front of me. I guessed she must be very poor, as although she looked well fed, her blouse was sadly short of buttons. The poor thing was also without the very necessary bra. I could tell she had not taken a course in manicuring as she kept dropping the file. With her blouse already flapping she bent down, dangerously risking the last lonely button. Fortunately her ampleness lost the fight to escape the shirt, but the restraining button was now stretched to cracking point.

While she searched for the file she clasped my hand firmly and squashed it to her knee. I had an uncomfortable amount of contact with a considerable amount of exposure. The third time she dropped the file her own nails were so short and bitten that she had extreme difficulty picking it up. She needed both hands so she left my hand pinioned between her breasts. I tried to look unconcerned as it was forced with her fumbling to rove from breast to breast. My cool veneer broke and I took this opportunity to escape. I snatched back my hand before it was rubbed raw by stiff nipples. I pretended I needed it to shield my embarrassed cough. The other three women seated around me smiled sweetly, apparently oblivious to anything untoward.

The barber looked round the corner at our happy group and decided that the manicure must be finished. Using a mixture of words and gestures he told me that Valerie would still be a while and so would I like a massage while I waited. He showed me the number of notes it would cost me, which was the equivalent of six pounds. I must admit I was feeling a bit stiff and six pounds seemed a very reasonable price. I asked, 'With whom?' He demonstrated that the blonde was the most experienced but I could have any or all of them.

I assumed the younger girls must be on a Bolivian masseuses' youth training scheme and they wanted to watch to learn the ropes. They might also be curious to see a foreigner and whether or not I might give them all a big tip.

I looked from one beautiful, smiling girl to the next, trying to make a choice. With four pairs of pert teenage breasts straining at me, the truth struck like a bolt of lightning.

'This was a brothel!'

These innocent-looking girls were ladies of the night and it was still only half-past three in the afternoon. The barber was suggesting I succumbed my innocent young body to four beautiful, bewitching, enticing, gorgeous, expert, heavenly nymphs.

Well I was horrified, naturally, but what should I do? The friendly young girls would take a refusal so personally. They may think that after inspecting what they had to offer, I was no longer interested. After two months' social starvation in the jungle, I was very interested. I certainly didn't want to upset anyone.

'It's one way of injecting my foreign currency into their beleaguered economy,' I considered, generously.

They crossed elegant tanned legs beneath short skirts and smoothed the wrinkles from tightly stretched clothing. Their red lips demanded a decision.

I did what any upstanding, considerate Englishman would do.

Chapter 11

*

Tarantula

As we marched up to the completed jungle house we tried to make as much noise as possible. Pumas are particularly fond of inhabiting abandoned huts. Given the opportunity they will run away when disturbed but cornered they might attack. We therefore tried to give plenty of warning of our approach. Fortunately there was no sign of pumas. Instead we were faced with a different problem. Inside the house at the base of the centre pole was a large blue egg.

Robin and Guy conferred. Valerie and I grumbled.

They decided, 'We can't stay in the house if a bird's nesting.'

We replied, 'Not even a chicken is stupid enough to lay an egg there.'

They studied their bird books. 'Tinamou lays four or five large blue eggs usually at base of tree.'

'Somebody's put it there,' we objected.

They took no notice. 'The Tinamou may think the pole is a tree.'

'So where are the rest of the eggs?' we countered.

'The egg is so central, it looks like a ceremonial offering.'

We left them to confer. Valerie pulled back the plastic sheeting where we stored our supplies. Inside there was a nest and a large tarantula. Valerie chased the tarantula until she had trapped it in a jar. The discovery of a nest finally made the decision.

'We'll just have to make camp on the other side of the stream.'

Valerie and I grumbled our objections. We had spent

two and a half months living in a bloody little tent. This
was the first time we could sleep in the completed house.
We were not happy.

Clemente arrived that afternoon and was surprised to
see we had pitched camp. Puzzled, he asked, 'Did you find
the egg?'

'You left it?'

'Yes, I found a nest down by the river.'

'What happened to the rest of the eggs?'

He smiled sheepishly, 'I don't know.'

He had eaten them. He pulled back the plastic and
kicked the nest out of the house. Robin was horrified.
'What are you doing?'

'It's a rat's nest,' he pronounced.

Valerie and I smiled smugly. We moved in.

Robin found a humming-bird nest only a few feet from
the house. It was so small it was built on a leaf stem. The
parent bird zipped around the camp. I could never get
used to the disproportionate racket this tiny bird made.
Its beating wings would whip the air making a loud whoop.
I would jump round expecting to look down a hungry
puma's throat. Instead there would be a three-inch metal-
lic-green blur as the bird returned to the nest.

Humming-birds beat their wings up to eighty times a
second. Their tiny hearts have to beat one thousand times
a minute to supply enough oxygen to run their energetic
muscles – even faster during mid-air mating. To fuel
this minute power pack, they have to feed every fifteen
minutes.

While Robin photographed the humming-bird we
searched for a curassow nest. After a few unsuccessful
days we gave up and decided to do a twenty-four-hour
population survey, taking six-hour shifts.

We made another hide within ten minutes' walking
distance from camp as we would need to get there in the
dark. We cut and marked a wide path to the hide. Straying
off into the jungle at night was not advisable. We made

the hide on top of a small hill so the sound of calls could reach us from all sides. We strapped the frame together with palm rope and started to cover it with palm leaves. We were attempting to make the hide lightproof so our candle wouldn't scare any of the birds. In one of the palm trees we disturbed a nest of night wasps. These large yellow and white wasps became so upset at our attacking them that I decided to retire to a convenient log. I left Guy and Valerie to burn out the nest and sadly they were stung repeatedly.

Clemente, Robin and Valerie left the park as Valerie had to prepare for her imminent departure for England. The curassow project money had run out months ago. Valerie and Guy had been surviving on private funds. Valerie was now penniless and this was forcing her back to England.

Guy and I started a night survey. I had the early evening stint of six until twelve. Armed with a flask of coffee, notebook, candle and machete, I wriggled through the leaves into my dank confine. We had swept the ground to make sure we were not sitting on anything too unpleasant. I had also put down a small piece of plastic sheeting to keep me off the damp earth. It was black in the den so I lit the candle and checked that no snakes had arrived in my absence. Reasonably satisfied, I sat back to start my vigil.

I logged very few calls and by half-past ten I was becoming a bit spooked by the eerie noises. All alone, the moonless jungle took on frightening possibilities. In my imagination I believed I provided an excellent opportunity for the Yuqui Indians to diversify into European cuisine. The fall of a leaf or the snap of a twig conjured up visions of poison darts and bubbling cooking pots. I forced myself to think of my family but the only faces I could see had vacant eyes and sharp white teeth. My nervousness amplified a distant rustle into stampede proportions. I was convinced something was out there. Maybe a jaguar waiting for me to stick my head out so he could bite it off.

My feeble candle was no comfort as it just cast hideous shadows. In its flickering, every branch appeared to be a large writhing snake.

Adding to my miseries was the discovery that we had made the hide on a beetle nursery. Every few seconds the ground would shudder and beetles would crawl out. They would fly suicidally at my candle flame. Their wings would crackle and melt and they would fall on to the wick. The candle would be snubbed out by their smouldering carcasses. I would be left groping desperately for matches before a new attack could be mounted. At one point so many beetles emerged, the ground trembled and the whole area seemed to quake.

I tucked my legs up under my chin in an attempt to squeeze my entire body off the infested area and back on to the small piece of plastic sheeting. Directly above my head there was a loud rustle. I fumbled for the machete and flicked on the torch. I could see nothing except the palm leaves of the roof. The fronds were still entwined like long green fingers reaching across the blackness.

The noise stopped. It's the wind, I told myself. It's a hideously poisonous snake, I thought. The rustling started again. Squashed into a ball I peered nervously at the roof. There was no denying the noise. Something was up above me.

I wiped my palm, my knuckles bone-white as I gripped the machete. The noise stopped. I imagined who or whatever was preparing for attack. I could do nothing but wait.

My heartbeat thumped in my ears, then it was drowned by another rustling, almost deafening in comparison. I jerked my head to stare for the source of the noise. The leaves parted and a silhouette of a hand-shape dropped. Directly above my eyes it fell, threatening to smother entirely my uplifted face. Instinct dropped my head and bunched my shoulders, readying for impact. It landed squarely on the top of my head. Instinct was still moving me forward and it slipped back, caressing my vulnerable

neck. My involuntary shiver shrugged it from the anchor-
age it had secured against my shirt collar and it dropped
down my back on to the plastic.

My machete had slashed before the beam of my torch
had found its target. Focused, it revealed a black tarantula
larger than my hand. My machete had accounted for two
of its hairy legs. They lay twitching beside it, as it waved its
gruesome stumps accusingly. Still in shock, my machete
swung again and again until only a minced pile of hairy
entrails lay twitching. I forced myself to stop and I took
my first breath for a minute. After filling my lungs I
carefully brushed out the pulsating mass which was
already attracting hungry insect scavengers.

I sat back on my stained plastic, heartbeat gradually
returning to normal. However, I could not relax. I stared
about me, jerking my head at the slightest sound. Twenty
minutes later I had recovered enough to pour myself a
coffee from my flask. I lifted the little cup to my lips.

Whack! something hit the wall of the hide.

The cup fell from my startled hand, the hot coffee
scalding my wedding tackle.

'Shit! What is it this time?'

It dropped down through the leaves in the wall. I could
see nothing. I waited, the coffee steam rising from my
trousers. There was a loud scrunching as something
crawled through the palm leaves. I directed my torch beam at
the sound, my machete already raised. The leaves parted and
the shape flew straight at the candle. The flame was snuffed
out with a sizzling of wings. I caught the crippled creature
in the faint torch beam and trapped it to the ground with
the machete blade. I lit the candle and studied my assailant.

It was a massive mantid, but a species I could not
identify. It was about eight inches long and its body was
bulbous and covered with what looked like brown fur. Its
sickle-shaped jaws were a couple of centimetres long. In
my apprehensive state of mind there was no mercy for
attacking insects. Although I chopped it in half, its power-

ful jaws still groped for something to bite. I fed it its own lower body. It clamped its mandibles around its own legs and attempted to crush them.

All this gruesome aggression was not doing my pulse rate any good and so I carefully shovelled the insect out to join the tarantula. I sat back on my battle-worn plastic and waited the hour and a half before I could return to camp.

We only had one torch so I would have to return to camp before Guy could relieve me. When the time came I was almost loath to leave. The hide was at least a flimsy protection against attack. Nothing could ambush me unprepared. Whatever the aggression, I would at least have some warning. The path back to the camp, however, was threatened from every direction by unseen horrors. I steeled myself and pushed my head out into the blackness. Wielding my machete I stood upright and walked stiffly forward.

It wasn't ordinary blackness. It was the blackness of the unknown, emphasizing my solitude and vulnerability. It had substance. It touched me.

I walked on, clamping down a dreadful urge to run. I sensed eyes everywhere, burning holes in my back. I tried to surprise them by firing my torch beam in a sweep of the night. I never caught anything. This should have reassured me but instead it convinced me of the cunning of my enemies. I couldn't even walk fast, as I could easily stumble off the path and walk for ten minutes without realizing I was lost. I caught sight of the campfire and let out a relieved sigh. Guy was sitting waiting for me.

'How was it?'

'Ah, no problems, a bit boring really.'

'OK, see you in six hours then.'

Off he marched. With only the two of us I was now alone in the camp, but tucked up in the womb of my sleeping bag I felt invulnerable.

We did four more nights in the night hide, logging the curassow calls. I started to get grey hairs.

At the end of our stint it began to rain and so we stayed in the house. We decided to wait a day before returning to Buena Vista. We still had plenty of supplies and the weather might break. I was volunteered to collect some water from the stream. Taking the container, I walked through the driving rain and knelt on the muddy shore, collecting as much leaf matter as water. I noticed movement in the dark stream.

It was the newt. I dropped the container and moved to a position to catch it. It disappeared under the surface. Standing in the murky waters I was soaked by the rain. However, I crouched down and waited. A couple of minutes later the newt popped its head up for air. I snatched out as it appeared, caught it firmly and lifted it up. It wasn't a newt, it was a lizard. This was even more exciting for I knew of no freshwater, totally aquatic, lizard. It was about five inches long with a slender grey body. Its belly was chequered with black and white scales. I rushed back to the camp with my prize.

'I've caught it!'

Guy immediately emptied a large jar of rice and we popped the lizard in. We had lived in this one spot for three months and nobody else had ever spotted the lizard. The only previous time I had seen it, it had also been raining, so I guessed they must become active in the rain. Convinced there must be more, I left Guy examining the lizard and went back down to the stream.

I sat for twenty minutes in the pelting rain studying the water. My patience was rewarded when I saw a little head bob up. Before I could reach it, it disappeared under a rock. I lifted the rock but it stayed submerged. I waited for about three minutes until it reappeared. I grabbed at it and plucked it from the water. This one was slightly larger than the other and it had orange speckles on its head and an orange tinge to its belly. I took it back to camp and left it with Guy.

I returned to the stream and sat for a further half an

hour. I was now shivering with cold and was completely drenched. Just about to give up, I caught sight of another lizard swimming in the shallow water. I cornered it against a tree root. This one was the largest and had the same colouring as the first. Its belly was very clearly swollen with eggs. I carefully carried this expectant mother back to camp.

Guy had not wasted time. He had filled the jar with mud, stones and twigs and poured in some water. The lizards didn't climb on to the twigs but instead they floated in the water. We studied them at length. I had clearly caught a juvenile, possibly a female, an adult male and a pregnant female. I was now faced with a dilemma. I knew that any I took back to Santa Cruz University would eventually be killed. Which, therefore, should be sacrificed in the name of science? The benefits of having a pregnant female would be considerable. It would immediately answer many of the reproduction questions if it was a new species. My conscience would not allow it. I took her back down to the river to release her. I tried to excuse my unscientific behaviour by telling myself that they were probably very common. On the other hand, if they were a new species, if I condemned her to death I might well wipe out the entire colony. I set her free and she swam off like a little alligator.

I spent the rest of the day collecting tiny spiders and dropping them into the jar. The lizards snapped them up greedily, unconcerned at their new restrictive home. The rain looked as if it was going to settle in for a few days so we decided to get back to Santa Cruz as soon as possible.

First thing the next morning we packed up and set off. The weather had brightened considerably but we still decided to leave. We walked down the first stretch of river, the lizards safely stowed in the dampened jar in my rucksack. I had removed most of the water and just left a little mud in the bottom.

We passed the tapir pool and in the bright morning

sunlight something red flashed in the river ahead. It looked like a fish as it shot around in the shallows. We ran up to it. The bright shape disappeared under a rock.

I knelt down and spotted two legs protruding from under the rock. It was a large frog that had wedged itself in the crevice. Guy tried to lift the boulder while I grabbed its body. It came out with a struggle. About five inches from nose to vent, it was a myriad of bright colours, red, orange, blue, green, white and black. But its most distinctive marking was one hundred formed in black numerals across its back. I held it while Guy looked for something to house it. My hand started to sting painfully. Guy held open a hiking sock and I stuffed it inside. I knotted the end and, satisfied it couldn't escape, I took out some soap and started to scrub my hand.

My hand was covered in insect-bite scars and scratches from barbed vines. The nasty secretions from the frog's skin had entered these abrasions and were playing merry hell with my nerves. My hand had swollen red and felt as if it was burning. I scrubbed with the soap, disregarding the pain, forcing the lather deep into my cuts. It was a very difficult procedure as I had to keep one foot resting lightly on the hiking sock which kept trying to hop away.

I didn't stop for five minutes. The secretions from frogs can be very toxic and in the case of poison arrow frogs they can prove fatal. The kokoi poison arrow frog of Colombia is the most poisonous animal in the world. It has been estimated that it would only take 0.0001 g. of its poison to kill a man. I hoped for the best.

We soaked the frog sock and put it into another jar with a little water. The pain in my hand gradually faded although I felt slightly nauseous for a couple of days afterwards. We walked out of the park, stopping frequently to moisten the collection of beasts in my rucksack.

CHAPTER 12

*

Water Lizards

A strange buzz of excitement greeted our return to Buena Vista. The normally lethargic locals were all standing around gesticulating and discussing something very animatedly. We were not able to understand their baffling exclamations. It appeared they were all comparing the dimensions of the one that got away. They shouted at each other: 'No, it was longer!' 'Rounder!' 'No, bigger than that!'

Whatever it was, the consensus was that it was big and that it had got away. They pointed at the sky and shrugged when we probed for an explanation. We set off for Robin's house, perhaps he could clarify this manifestation of flying fish.

He was just as excited as the locals. What they had seen was no heavenly salmon. There had been a UFO.

Guy and I laughed, incredulous. Robin became quite indignant. He stuck out his chin and explained what he had seen.

At about nine-thirty two nights before, he and Valerie had been sitting in his garden sipping a crate of beer. In the corner of his eye he noticed a perfectly round cloud. He turned to study it more closely. It was spherical but it also had a perfect circle in its centre. This core beamed like a spotlight.

The object was moving in the opposite direction to the clouds, at a constant speed. Robin had run for his binoculars. With further intensification, the UFO's edges were still smooth and crisp. The object could not be natural. They watched it cross the sky for five minutes until it vanished. It had not faded away or disappeared behind the horizon. It had just evaporated in an instant.

With increased understanding we quizzed the other members of the village. The story was repeated exactly by all. Almost everyone had seen it as most people sit out in the warm evenings. It was also reported in the papers. It had been sighted as far away as La Paz and Santiago in Chile.

Nobody could offer an explanation. Even the papers just reported the sighting without any attempt to solve the mystery. Well, naturally I was disappointed. A chance of a lifetime to see a UFO and I had been under the bloody trees in the jungle.

At least I had the consolation of catching my water lizards and their hungry little bellies demanded my attention. We gave them a temporary home in the dangerous pets' corner with the one hundred frog, Valerie's tarantula and Oscar, a curly-tailed iguana. Oscar had been given to us by a local who had found him in a felled tree.

That evening I caught some little insects for the animals' dinner. Oscar was mostly vegetarian so he had mango. I was just dropping a spider into the water lizards' jar when I noticed the male wasn't there. I checked under the twigs, searching frantically. He'd escaped, my new species had done a runner!

I looked forlornly along the bench but there was no sign, he was long gone. I cracked open a consolatory bottle of beer and dropped the bottle top in the bucket bin. Something moved. I looked down and there sitting pompously on the pungent pile of mango stones, eggshells and bottle tops, was the water lizard. He must have scuttled along the bench and dropped into the bucket. The steep plastic sides had held him captive. I breathed a very amateur herpetologist sigh of relief. Lizard eyed me suspiciously as I fished him out and put him back into his jar. I secured the top with two extra loops of string while he paddled around, rather satisfied with his short holiday.

The following afternoon the cleaner accidentally released Valeric's tarantula and it hid in the dark corners of the house. The next morning it appeared from under my sofa just as I was putting on my socks. Following my recent jungle tarantula experience, I jumped ten feet.

After a couple of days recovering, I got a lift with the priests to Santa Cruz. They dropped me and my collection of wildlife in the central plaza. Ladened down with interesting opaque cartons, I caught a taxi to the university.

From the car I noticed a lame horse limping in the central grass reserve. It was trapped on each side by streams of traffic. As we drew closer it stumbled forward, catching its dangling hoof on the ground. Its knee bent open, exposing the complete bone joint. The taxi driver observing my horrified stare took the opportunity to instruct me.

'It's been knocked over.'

'Why doesn't somebody shoot it?' I whispered.

'It will die soon enough.'

We drove on. I stared back at the crippled beast, sickened at my impotence to relieve its pain and the lack of interest shown by my fellow commuters.

'It happens all the time. They're too old to work, too old to eat. No one can afford to shoot them, so they turn them loose.'

I was dropped at the university and I poured out to Paolo what I had just seen. I said we should do something, get a gun, shoot it. He told me there was nothing we could do. It probably had massive internal injuries. It would be reacting on instinct and was probably beyond pain. He said if we shot it the owners would arrive and accuse us of killing their perfectly healthy horse. They would be able to produce witnesses as everyone likes an opportunity to screw the gringos. We would end up in court paying huge damages. 'Forget it. It will probably be dead by now.'

I gave him the frog and went to sit under a tree for a cigarette. I found the brutality of Bolivia unacceptable. When I returned a large crowd was standing around Paolo as he and his trainee attempted to photograph my frog. Everyone was very excited as no one recognized it. It was reported in the papers the next day as, 'One hundred Frog. Possible new species found in Amboro.'

When the crowds left I asked Paolo what he was going to do with it. He phrased it tactfully as he knew I didn't like to kill things. 'We'll preserve it.'

'I'd prefer you did it now than have it sitting in a tank for days waiting to die.'

I held the frog as Paolo's trainee injected cyanide into its heart. It took a double dose as the frog just wouldn't die. I was glad I had released my expectant mother water lizard.

When the excitement of the one hundred frog had blown over, I took Paolo aside. 'I've got something else for you.'

My excitement was infectious as his eyes twinkled with anticipation. 'What?'

'The newts.'

'You caught them?'

'Yes, but they're not newts, they're lizards.'

'No?'

'Yes, and I've got two.'

'*Magnífico!*'

We put them in a tank with a couple of inches of water and a few rocks. They swam around, glad of the extra space. We dropped in a few spiders and as soon as they hit the water the lizards gobbled them up. Paolo gave one of his trusted students the job of feeding them and recording their behaviour.

'Their lives are your responsibility, Paolo. I just caught them.'

*

CHAPTER 13

Vampires

It was Valerie's last few days before she returned to England. I didn't know what I was going to do without her. Through the shared suffering and hardships of the jungle we had become very close. She was a sister to me. Her beauty regularly tempted me but surprisingly I was able to stay in control. I must have respected her.

We decided to have a feast to see her off. She agreed to a controlled cull of the chicken flock. She had taken a long time to come round to this as she was very fond of her brood. She had, after all, had them since they were eggs. However, she realized that the minute she was gone Guy and I would eat them anyway.

We had had many shooting competitions with the air rifle. We had used mangos, avocados, bottle tops and gourds on the gourd tree as our targets. Our favourite was a saucepan lid. With a direct hit it would make a very satisfying clunk.

Guy, a crackshot and the undisputed champion of our shooting competitions, was given the job of executioner. He took the air rifle and went out on to the porch. Sitting in a chair with the gun resting on his knee, he threw out a handful of corn and called the chickens. They arrived clucking and started to scratch for the grain. Valerie looked mournfully at the flock, deciding which should be sacrificed. Of the eleven young chickens, five were cockerels. Sooner or later they would fight for supremacy over the flock. Valerie therefore chose the smallest cock. Three months of near starvation had made us hard. Guy sighted the gun, took careful aim and squeezed the trigger. He had aimed for its eye. The cockerel looked up, squawked and ran off.

'Damn, missed!' Valerie nominated another cockerel. The gun kicked out another pellet.

'Missed again!'

The third time Guy coaxed a greedy cockerel with more corn until it was only six feet away. Pop, the bird keeled over and lay flapping in the dirt. I went to pick it up. The other chickens finally caught on they were being shot at and scarpered into the undergrowth.

As I walked out into the garden I noticed another maimed cockerel lying in the grass. It was the first victim, so Guy had hit it after all. I looked for the second cockerel and true enough I spotted it under a bush. He had hit all three. One by one I stretched their necks over my knee as I had seen my Bolivian neighbours do. The vertebrae of their necks popped apart, killing them instantaneously. I felt no pity or remorse, just hunger. We hung them on the grapefruit tree to let the blood drip off. They were bleeding rather badly and I managed to stain my Fred Flintstone boxer shorts. We were now stuck with a thrace of cockerels. With no fridge or freezer available we were going to have to eat them all. It would take a lot of beer to wash down this amount of stringy flesh.

We drew straws to decide who would do the beer run – I lost. I was going to need a horse. I picked up our blue nylon horse rope and went out into the garden to find one. We had three horses on the estate. They belonged to a man in the village. The arrangement was that he could keep his horses in our garden provided that he kept our fence in order and we could ride them.

The horses had other ideas and these certainly did not include letting large foreigners sit on their backs. The easiest horse to catch was called Migraine. Valerie had christened him this because he was perhaps as ugly and close to death a horse could look and still stand. Migraine had one particularly annoying habit. At night he would stroll on to the tiled porch and stamp his hooves. I could never understand why he did this unless he believed he was a chicken. The chickens were still sleeping in a huddle on the porch and the hen house now lay derelict. Migraine would keep stamping his hooves until I charged out wielding a broom. A few nights of this and homemade horse-burger recipes featured regularly in my thoughts.

The next-best horse was a frisky little number Valerie had called Cheese. He was small but extremely fast and very difficult to catch. The third had two names: firstly we called him The Other One. When he couldn't remember we had christened him The Other One, we would call him Big Horse, because he was. He was the fastest and the hardest to catch. I was the Whitehouse professional horse catcher but I had never managed to catch Big Horse.

For my first tactic I tried the friendly approach. With the nylon rope stuffed down the back of my trousers I walked forward, my clenched hand proferred with unimaginable goodies. They were as trusting as Christmas Eve turkeys and galloped off to the other end of the garden. I gave up the softly, softly and chased Cheese and Big Horse around the field for about half an hour, trying to lasso them. My limp noose kept snagging on branches and never came closer than their departing rumps. As usual I gave up and caught Migraine, who was wheezing under a mango tree.

Although easy to catch, Migraine was not easy to move. He looked half mule and he was so stubborn you had to threaten him with a very large branch. We didn't have a saddle or reins, so while Valerie held him I climbed on to his bony back. I pointed him in the right direction and said 'Giddy up!'

He didn't respond. He had clearly not attended any international dressage competitions. I threatened him with the five-foot branch and he finally agreed to move. He sauntered at his own pace, not interested in my horsey encouragements. We mosied on up to town.

After half an hour and a couple of grass-eating diversions, we made it to Pablo's saloon. I tied Migraine to the corral and strode through the doorway. There were no other desperados in town. I hollered for six bottles of beer on the rocks. Nobody moved. I helped myself from the fridge and loaded the bottles into my saddlebag. 'Put it on the slate, barman.' Vaulting on to my trusty steed I shouted, '*Adiós, amigo*,' and rode off into the sunset.

Migraine ambled to a patch of luscious grass and stopped for a snack. Pablo passed me my stick and pushed Migraine round until he was pointing back towards the Whitehouse. He slapped his rump and Migraine bolted down the track. I dropped the stick and held on for dear life. In one hand I held a heavy bag of beer bottles and in the other I clutched a fistful of Migraine's mane. Fortunately he tired quickly and settled back into his steady gait. We made it to the Whitehouse before nightfall but I was severely damaged. Migraine's sharp bony back had bruised me and taken all the skin from my bum.

The excellent meal was little consolation. We invited Dennis, the trainee priest. He spent a lot of time with us in the brief periods we were out of the park. We were all roughly the same age and being English speakers naturally brought us together.

Dennis had fallen in love with Valerie. His love manifested itself in several ways: he talked about her all the time, he stared at her with his mouth open, he told her she was unique and he said that if he hadn't decided to be a priest he would want to marry her. They were all fairly subtle clues but taken together they could only spell one thing – the 'L' word.

She was very flattered that she had aroused a celibate. Guy and I tried to keep her feet on the ground by reminding her of Dennis's lack of female experience. The only thing the women of the corn fields of Iowa, from where he sprouted, could say was, 'Can I drive the combine harvester?'

Any woman who held an opinion, even on knitting patterns, would be a novelty to him. The wicked streak in her nature was tempted to seduce him but her Catholic upbringing kept her in check.

We had affected Dennis in another way. Unfortunately some of our bad language started to rub off on him. While eating the chickens I was particularly shocked when he twice said, 'Bugger me!'

If you consider the connotations of this word, it's jolly impolite. Dennis-the-Pure was saying it without the slightest hesitation. It seemed totally out of character. I asked him if he understood what he was saying. He looked surprised that I should be interested. I knew there must be some misunderstanding. I explained the origins of the word. Dennis turned white and was horrified. 'I've said that in front of the nuns,' he informed us.

Guy and Valerie were now on the floor in hysterics. What he thought we'd been saying was, 'Burger me.' In the context of, 'What a fool I am. Mince me, fry me up and put me in a bap.'

The English pronunciation had foxed him. As Winston Churchill said, 'Two nations divided by a common language.' I could only presume Dennis had grown up on Walton's mountain with Jim-Bob, John-Boy and Lizbeth. It was a hell of a party.

We saw Valerie off down in Santa Cruz. She would be back in England for Christmas and I almost envied her. We were very sad to see her go. I seemed to spend my life saying goodbye to people.

I popped in to the museum to see my lizards. They were still thriving and Paolo was accumulating photographs and data on their habits. I told him when the wet season started I would be leaving for a short trip around South America. If he felt it best to 'preserve them', it was up to him.

Guy and I went back into the park. This trip we concentrated on finding a curassow nest. We searched the study site systematically, every morning from six until twelve. We would return to camp and have some bread and tea and then start the search again until about four in the afternoon. We were not getting anywhere. There were no signs of any nest. We were grateful for the completed house as the weather turned wet. It rained briefly each evening but under the solid shelter of our house we avoided the worst of the weather.

I would gladly have spent the time just sitting in the house ruminating. But Guy's dedication to the curassow project kept us out searching against all the odds. Our silent tracking was occasionally rewarded when we would catch glimpses of humming-birds collecting spiders' webs to line their nests. This was a dangerous task as a tarantula could easily overpower the dainty birds.

On our fourth day we were battling up the steep mountain jungle following the curassow call. Vines, thorns and tree roots grasped and snagged across our path as if in some organic conspiracy to prevent our progress. We struggled on, ripping clothes and flesh on the assailing vegetation. Perilously clinging tree roots were often our only footholds in the mud-greased rainforest.

The mesmerizing notes of the curassow beckoned us. The magnetism of our elusive pied piper allowed us no rest. We were lured on, the slopes dropping away either side of our beguiled steps.

Scaling to a summit we worked our way along a ridge, crowded with trees. Sunlight from a clearing lengthened the shadows as we drew nearer. We broke out into the open. The clearing was the aftermath of a recent rockfall. Half the mountain had collapsed into the valley, plunging ancient trees and undergrowth over a precipice. A shingle moonscape was the resulting scar.

Guy and I forgot the curassow call and sat down on a rock for a cigarette. Resting, we searched the skies for the

rare condor. This, the largest bird of prey with a wingspan
of over ten feet, had only been spotted once in Amboro.
Instead, spiralling in the thermals were the ever-present
turkey vultures. Searching for carrion, they circled expectantly above us.

The curassow was still calling, its boom rolling through
the treetops. We took a couple of practise steps on the
steep shingle slope. We slipped slightly but our feet found
enough purchase to scramble on. To turn back would
mean losing the curassow and having to retrace our steps
along the ridge. We decided to risk the crossing.

With each stride we slid a couple of feet further down
the rockfall. Halfway across we stopped to assess our
situation. The exertion of digging into the almost fluid
gravel had taken its toll. We were both sweating and
breathing heavily. Balanced in the middle of the clearing
we were surprised how far down we had fallen. If we
carried on with this trajectory it was uncertain whether
we would make the sanctuary of the trees. Now closer to
the precipice, it was clear that if we toppled over the edge
the vultures would need a dustpan and brush to collect
our shattered remains.

I shot a nervous glance at the sky. The vultures were
circling lower. There was no point turning back. I had no
preference which side of the cliff I went over. Crouching,
we scrambled on, digging our fingers into the pebbles to
slow our slither. However, our fatigue was hindering us.
The edge was looming, the safety of the trees still twenty
feet away. Another couple of steps and we slipped five
feet. The displaced pebbles dropped silently over the edge.
Seconds later a shower of cracks echoed back as they hit
the valley floor.

Standing still we started to slip. We had to move. We
threw caution to the winds and ran for the trees. Our
bounds sent sprays of rocks over the edge until the whole
valley was filled with their resonant clattering.

Guy grabbed for a tree root and I grabbed for Guy.

Clutching the tree we hauled ourselves away from the edge. We sat down on the tree wheezing, my pulse thumping in my ears. The curassow let out another rhythm of notes but the hypnotism had been shattered. At that moment I would have taken great pleasure in eating the bird raw with just a splodge of cranberry sauce.

Guy stood up to follow the call. I was forced to follow. We never found the bloody turkey.

After an unsuccessful week's nest hunting we ran out of supplies so we started the trek out. We sped-marched with the skies rumbling ominously and didn't stop until we reached the farm of Mrs Arnaldo. She greeted us with her customary warmth and invited us into her hut. She boiled coffee and offered us a banana. Reclining in a hammock, her wellingtons dangling from her ballgown she told us the wrath of God would blast all sinners from the face of the earth. Sinners were poor people who didn't even have one horse – she had two.

Guy noticed that she had cloves of garlic on the window sill. I looked around. She had cloves by every window and hung on the door. 'They keep away the vampire bats. Don't you have any?' she asked amazed. When we replied we didn't, she became quite insistent that we take some. 'You never carry it in with you?' she asked, incredulous.

'Only to eat.'

She stuffed two cloves into my pocket. She grasped my hand, and filled with sincerity, she pleaded with me, 'Always keep it with you. It will protect you.' I promised I would. I offered her a cigarette and she took three for later. Saying our goodbyes we set off.

We sped-marched again, trotting along – almost jogging. Guy had slight asthma and therefore his fitness was a tremendous achievement. He led the whole way, driving me on through all fatigue. We made the edge of the park, cutting hours off previous exit times. Although he didn't admit it, I knew he felt as good as me about our physical achievement. He allowed me this much of a clue, 'It's good you don't want to stop all the time. It's much better to keep going.'

I nodded my agreement. We were crusty.

There was only one last trip into the park planned before the expected wet season. My body was now covered in fungus and insect bites. I was looking forward to a rest.

Dennis and I decided to have a short tour around South America. We started to plan our trip. He wanted to go and see Foz do Iguaçu in Brazil. He told me they are huge waterfalls. Iguaçu is a massive river that flows along the border of Brazil, Argentina and Paraguay. We decided to leave after Christmas with the Foz do Iguaçu our first objective.

*

CHAPTER 14

Christmas

Guy and Paolo went into the park and I was due to meet them there. I was waiting for two visiting Spanish ornithologists to arrive who I was to escort up to the study site. I had expected to take them two days after Guy's departure but they didn't appear. With little or no communication with Santa Cruz we couldn't discover what had happened to them. They eventually arrived, at midday, two days later. I wasn't prepared to take them in until first thing the following morning. That night there was a horrendous storm and in the morning it still hadn't blown over, so the trip was called off and the Spaniards disappeared back to Santa Cruz. I was greatly relieved as I was feeling ill with grippe, Bolivian flu. I had three horses and eight chickens to keep me company. Five Christmas cards had also managed to find their way through.

On Christmas Eve Robin came round and said we would have an evening meal at his house. I offered one of Valerie's chickens. I went out on to the porch with some corn and called for volunteers. The hens charged expectantly towards me so I threw the corn and sat down. They pecked away furiously, unaware that I had levelled the gun and was taking careful aim. I sighted a young rooster on the edge of the flock. As he came within range he looked up baffled as the rifle pellet blew away the back of his head. He scampered a few steps and then flopped over. Robin had now turned completely white and looked on the verge of vomiting. I broke the still flapping chicken's neck, just to make sure it was dead, and tied it to a tree to let the blood drip off. When the bird was reasonably dry Robin drove off with it in the back of his Land Rover and told me to come round at eight o'clock.

I spent the rest of the afternoon making three paper hats and looking at my Christmas cards. Again I was grateful for my Swiss Army penknife. With the scissors I cunningly crafted some party accessories out of pages of my notebook, wrote our names on the hats, then walked up in the dark to Robin's house. He'd got the beer in and the chicken had been cooked in next door's underground wood oven. Miriam, Robin and I sat around his table, wearing paper hats and eating the orange rooster. He was surprisingly big and tender. He had done us proud and we washed him down with some red wine. I sat back fully satisfied. After a few more beers I left Robin to his private party and walked up to the plaza.

The whole town was at midnight Mass and some people had made the long trek in from distant farms. I'd been invited to have midnight breakfast at the priesthood. I sat outside the church, as the whole town prayed, and foolishly waited at the door for the last five minutes of the service. At twelve the throngs began to file out. Most of them clearly believed I was a padre for they formed a long patient queue to shake my hand and wish me a happy Christmas. Dennis stood on the other side of the door also shaking hands. He looked over with a rueful smile, unprepared to rescue me, and I was forced to continue shaking the hands of these devoted peasants.

One by one they respectfully grasped my hand and shyly sought my greeting, 'Happy Christmas, Padre, and may God be with you.'

'Yes, and the same to you.'

Looking down my line it appeared that no one was prepared to leave the church until they had met me. Fortunately no one asked me to bless their new-born children.

I had the vague impression that one toothless old crone
had rejoined the back of the queue for another kiss. I
escaped and left my last few diehards forlorn. I ushered
them out on the pretext that I had to help lock the church
doors.

We switched off the lights and walked into the priest's
house. Inside were padres Paul and Tom and the two
nuns, Anne-Shirley and Melanie. After a short prayer we
all sat round the table eating bacon and eggs and drinking
tea. Melanie had also made some cakes.

'I haven't seen you at mass, Oliver.'

'No, I'm not a Catholic.'

'Oh, really, what are you?'

'More bacon anyone?'

'Oh, yes please.'

'You were saying, Oliver.'

'Urm, well, I'm not really anything.'

'You do believe in God?'

'Well, I try to live by Christian morals.'

'Could I trouble you for the butter?'

'There you go.'

'Thank you.'

'So you live by Christian morals?'

'Oh, yes, thou shalt not kill or covet thy neighbour's
wife . . . and all that.'

'Very laudable.'

'Thank you, although I have been tempted.'

'Umm, but you don't actually believe in God?'

'Well, not as such. Lovely tea, is it Earl Grey?'

'Yes, an English priest left it when he visited earlier this
year.'

'We English love our tea. I even take it into the park.'

'Why don't you believe in God, Oliver?'

'Err, well at this stage in my life, I find the concept of
God hard to comprehend.'

General murmurs of discontent.

'That's not to say I won't change. I certainly haven't

got a closed mind on the subject. Actually my mother's very religious.'

I sipped my tea, hoping for an interruption. None came.

'Yes, at one time she even thought about becoming a nun. But I'm rather glad she didn't.'

Silence.

'Well, I wouldn't be here, would I?'

Pleading, 'Can I help with the washing-up?'

'No, No, you're a guest.'

'So why have you turned away from God, Oliver?'

'Ah, I wouldn't say I'd turned away, more like pulled into a lay-by for a while.'

'A lay-by?'

I gulped down my last mouthful of fried egg and stood up.

'Yes, well, it's been a lovely breakfast but I really must be off. Thanks for inviting me and err, Happy Christmas!'

'Happy Christmas and may God bless you.'

'That would be jolly nice.' I edged towards the door.

'I shall pray for you, Oliver.'

'Super, that's marvellous, goodnight.'

In unison, 'Goodnight!'

The door slammed behind me as I strolled out on to the plaza. I lit a cigarette and drew heavily. I was suffering post-Spanish Inquisition trauma.

A group of the local youth were sitting under the plaza trees in the warm evening. I went to join them. As if by unanimous plotting a seat was made available for me next to Anita. I had seen her from a distance a number of times in the last few weeks but we had not spoken since the graduation. She seemed to have an inexhaustible supply of short skirts. That night was no exception, the white material contrasting with her tanned legs. Charo invited me to go with her and her sister to a party. Anita looked at me, waiting for my decision. The mischievous con- fidence was gone; instead her eyes had an unsure vul- nerability that I found even more bewitching. I played hard to get and managed to delay my answer for nearly ten seconds. We walked about three kilometres to a chicken farm.

There was no party: just a few drunken relatives. I sat looking at the stars and dreamt of England. Although Anita constantly served me with drink, I longed for bed.

Everyone finally piled into a lorry which took us back to Buena Vista. I stood on my own at the back of the lorry, but Anita managed to edge perceptibly closer with every lurch of the unstable vehicle. Her short skirt was constantly whipped up by the wind and this rather brought my attention to her otherwise subtle advance. I retreated to the corner, but she now had the scent and approached remorselessly. She took full advantage of a particularly violent lurch as we struck a crater pothole and covered the last metre in one elegant stumble. I hadn't the heart to let her fall after all this effort. I caught her at the last moment and pulled her firmly upright. Another lurch squashed us together up against the side of the vehicle. My pulse thumped as I felt her nubile form pressed against my abstinent flesh. She looked up at me in this intimate embrace, suitably grateful for my assistance. I wondered how grateful. Probably married-first grateful. Still holding her round the waist with my free hand, I lifted her chin. She succumbed pleasantly and so I lowered my lips to plant number one. Her long eyelashes lowered expectantly, but on my final approach the lorry screamed to a shuddering halt and pitched us stumbling to the front.

I jumped down and lifted her slowly to the ground. Still holding her, I again lifted her chin and she responded, puckering her moistened lips. After a few seconds and still no kiss, she opened her eyes to find out the delay.

I smiled, kissed her nose and said 'Happy Christmas'. I untangled myself from her clasp and set off for the Whitehouse, chuckling at this new height of wickedness. Ever the optimist, I was confident this cruel titillation would pay dividends. It wasn't as rotten as it sounds as

I'd been conscious of a dozen eyes watching us. Also, although my understanding of Spanish was fairly good, my conversation was generally confined to short phrases. 'Let's find a Ford Transit where we can be alone,' was therefore out of my linguistic reach.

Walking home in the bright moonlight of half-past three on Christmas morning, I decided to make a special effort to improve my Spanish. It was clear it was going to be a long and arduous journey to satisfaction in this romance.

I stayed on the sofa until five o'clock Christmas Day. The beer and late night had not helped my body combat the onset of grippe. I had hoped to have a cheese omelette for Christmas dinner but as I grated the cheese a couple of maggots crawled out on to my hand. Instead I boiled my single egg and in the growing darkness I lit my last candle. I switched on the tape recorder and tucked into my candlelit dinner for one. The egg was slightly hard boiled but the cockroaches didn't seem to mind. They scuttled round my plate stealing away the tiniest morsel. I left them to it and leant back on the stool to listen to my Christmas tape. My mother had sent me a tape full of messages from each member of my large family. It had arrived in Santa Cruz just in time for Christmas. A tear came to my eye as my cousin's three-year-old daughter sang me 'jingle bells' and then was prompted by her mummy, 'Say "Happy Christmas" to Oliver.'

She had whispered, 'Happy Birffday, Oliver.' After approximately the sixth re-play in two days my stereo batteries finally packed up.

I sat silent at the table in the flickering candlelight re-reading my five Christmas cards with the cockroaches my only company. I couldn't make a cup of coffee as the water had been turned off. The authorities couldn't afford the fuel to work the pump. The water went off every night at seven but it had been off for two days already and my reserve bucket was getting so low that I daren't spare any.

Although I had made my egg last nearly half an hour I

was still not satisfied. My feverish mind started to lust after food and I quickly fell into a daydream stupor. I predictably started with turkey and considered every ingredient of each course so meticulously that it was nine o'clock before I finished my third helping of mince pies and brandy butter. Noticing the time I came out of my repose and wondered where Dennis was. He had promised to visit, but he had still not arrived. I decided I wasn't well enough to walk up to the plaza. I climbed stiffly off the stool and hobbled to the sofa, resigned that this Christmas would be personless as well as presentless. I was just drifting back into my starvation fever and trying to decide whether to have the brie or the stilton when a knock roused me. My candle had burned out so I groped in the dark for the door. It was padre Paul. Dennis had been waiting for a phone call from his family all day and had not dared leave the phone. As soon as padre had finished his heavy religious duties he had driven down to collect me. These people were so considerate. I left behind my Christmas cards and we drove up to the priest's house.

I stayed for an hour and ate a few of their food scraps. They didn't have cockroaches. Fortified with food I felt in need of entertainment. I strolled out into the plaza where I spotted Anita sitting with her friends, wearing a provocative little number. I moved in, took her by the hand and led her into the dark. Before you could say 'mouth to mouth', I was practising resuscitation. Sadly she wouldn't allow me to check under her blouse for her heartbeat.

However, satisfied with my bronze award revival technique, I walked her home and returned to the Whitehouse. Clearly silver and gold awards were going to take long-term dedication.

The grippe was debilitating so I stayed in bed. Guy and Paolo returned on Boxing Day. They'd very nearly been washed out and had spent six hours fighting down a stretch of river that should only have taken two hours. For

Christmas dinner they had eaten better than I had. They had fried grubs in garlic.

Anita was unhappy that I hadn't been up to see her and she persuaded some of the locals to drive down on a tractor. She popped in and I grappled briefly but unsuccessfully. She evaded my lecherous clutches like a flighty nymph. She knew enough slips to suggest she had a black belt in octopus wrestling. She skipped off pertly. I was left with only my fever to cuddle.

The next few days I was ill and stayed on my sofa all day to make sure I was rested enough in the evenings to re-embark on operation 'Anita'. Dennis and I had to put off our departure date until I was recovered.

On New Year's Day Robin came round. He didn't look happy and this was confirmed as he sat down. 'Anyone say "Happy New Year" and I'll punch them.' He'd accidentally run over and killed his neighbour's dog.

CHAPTER 15

*

Yellow Fever

At the beginning of January I kissed Anita goodbye with a promise I would buy her something from Brazil and I set off for Santa Cruz. I hoped absence would make her heart grow more accessible as I'd nearly exhausted my repertoire of sudden movements.

The micro buses were packed with people returning to work after the Christmas break. I decided to hitch a lift. There was very little other traffic on the road but after an hour a huge lorry stopped. I climbed on to the back and sat on ten tons of rock. I was still in my New Year spirit and had forgotten to ask the driver how much he would charge for this lift. I sat in the wind and driving rain, just happy to be off travelling again. The driver charged me a ridiculous sum, about two pounds, but I was not in the mood to argue. I would be in Santa Cruz for a few days before Dennis arrived, so I booked into the cheapest but cleanest hotel I could find.

After unpacking my toothbrush I was just settling down to an afternoon siesta when the phone rang. The receptionist told me two men from Immigration wanted to see me. Annoyed at being disturbed I asked her what they wanted.

'They want to check your passport.'

Slightly indignant that my passport should be open for general inspection, I replied with as much British subject under the protection of her Majesty's Secretary of State for Foreign and Commonwealth Affairs as I could stoke into my voice.

'I'll be down in ten minutes.'

The receptionist suggested, 'You'd better come quickly, they don't like to be kept waiting.'

'I'll be down in five minutes,' I stated firmly, replacing the receiver. Many people had told me rumours of bogus immigration men but I was sceptical. However, it seemed sensible to meet them at the busy reception rather than alone in my room. I double checked I'd locked the door, as thoughts of unwelcome visitors popped into my mind.

Two minutes later, clutching my passport, I went down stairs. The two men were leaning against the reception desk, chatting. They wore smart casual clothes in pastel pinks, greens and yellows, and flaunted their wealth with gold rings and watches. I stood behind them like a dis-obedient schoolboy waiting for their attention. They made no sign of noticing my presence so I boldly said *'Buenas tardes.'* They turned and gave me a polite good afternoon. Politeness seemed as good a policy as any, so I shook hands with both of them.

They took my passport and meticulously studied it, comparing me with my photo and checking the validity of each stamp. They asked me procedural questions like my name, where I was living and what I was doing in Bolivia. They asked these questions with courtesy, although they gave the impression they didn't believe my answers. They asked me what I was doing in Santa Cruz. I said I was visiting friends. I knew if I mentioned my trip it would only lead to more questions. They smiled at my answer, as if we were sharing a joke. Apparently satisfied they handed back my passport, turned on their Italian-made heels and left. I sighed my relief, as it had been a con-siderable strain on my limited Spanish. I asked the recep-tionist if she knew them. She nodded and said one word, 'Interpol.'

The word jarred my brain.

'Interpol?' The receptionist made herself busy. She had no intention of answering further questions. Her experience knew no virtuous foreigners. To her I was just another cocaine gringo.

Interpol by popular rumour was one of the most feared regimes in South America. I had heard they could go anywhere and do anything. Stories of their corruption were legendary. This wasn't the Interpol of the West. It was Interpol South American style; powerful, faceless and corrupt. The fact that I was innocent of all crimes did nothing to alleviate the guilt I now felt. I searched my past looking for a felonious skeleton. I hadn't even got a parking ticket in my irreproachable closet. I became aware of disturbing questions.

'Where had they got my name?'

'Was it just a random checking of foreigners?'

'Were they looking for me specifically?'

I started to feel increasingly vulnerable in my solitude. In the mounting paranoia I searched my room for any alien substances which might have arrived in my brief absence. Finding nothing, I forced out a laugh at my fears and went for a more than medicinal drink.

The next day I went to live at the Santa Cruz priest's house with Dennis.

We went together to a travel agent as Dennis needed a visa to enter Brazil. The travel agent told me I would need a yellow fever certificate to cross the Brazilian border. I'd already had the inoculation before leaving England, but somewhere along the way I'd lost my certificate. There was nothing for it, I'd have to get another jab. The travel agent told me the address of the medical centre and when he thought it was open.

I found the clinic and to my surprise it would start doing inoculations only two hours later than advertised. The building was a two-storey disaster area. The walls had once been plastered but the plaster now lay heaped around the old brick courtyard. I didn't have time to prepare myself for the predictably confusing clerical routine necessary to get a jab; with my visa running out, I would just have to hope it could all be done in a day. I returned at the appropriate time and searched all around the building. No one knew where I could get an inoculation.

Quite by chance as I looked down from the rusty balcony I spotted a woman carrying her screaming child from a basement building. She was holding a pad to his arm. My curiosity aroused, I went down to investigate. Inside the unplastered, brick-floored and doorless shed sat a large woman on a swivel chair. She said she could give me an injection but I would first need to register. In an amazing fit of helpfulness she directed me to the registration department who was sitting behind a plank of wood propped up on a pile of bricks. The registration gargoyle gave me half a ticket with a feeble attempt at spelling my name.

I cleared some rubble from a step and sat down until my number was called. Two children accompanied by their mother were heard to scream. They left the dark shed white faced, their eyes wide with fear and dripping with tears. And then it was my turn.

I walked bravely into the gloom. The nurse-like woman looked up from her desk and asked which injection I would like. I said yellow fever. She swung round and opened her small fridge. The green fridge light bathed her in ghoulish shadow. I watched her fingering various transparent tubes until she selected a full syringe. I had meanwhile rolled up my sleeve and she wiped my arm with a piece of grey cottonwool. On her desk was an old wooden test-tube rack stacked with varying sizes of needles. They were not sealed and I eyed them sceptically considering the squalor around me. Before I could react, she stuck the syringe into an unnecessarily large needle, withdrew it from the rack and stabbed it down on my arm, pressing the plunger. The force of the jab sunk the needle nearly an inch into my flesh but the syringe popped out. She tried to do it so fast that she automatically squirted half the drug before she could drop her downstroke. The yellow fever antidote jetted directly into my eye and then as the pressure on the syringe stopped the jet trickled all the way down my chest to my knee. The needle, however, was still imbedded firmly in my arm. The nurse apologized, thinking that it was actually quite amusing. Having three sisters in the trade, I reacted rather badly to her incredible incompetence. I wiped the liquid out of my eye and told her she was a bloody disgrace. She sat rather sheepishly. I didn't want to die of Aids so there was no way I was risking another of her needles. I told her to get on with it. She slotted the syringe back into the implanted needle and gave me the last third of injection. After she had signed my ticket I told her she was a stupid woman.

I went to get my certificate. Up on the balcony I found a likely looking queue. I noticed that I paid twice the fee that the woman in front of me had paid. I'd become used to this unofficial, three-tiered price system. There is a price for locals, a price for other South Americans and a price for gringos. For the sake of a few pounds it's not worth arguing. They gave me a certificate. We would collect Dennis's visa that afternoon and we would be ready to be off. I had only four days left on my visa.

*

CHAPTER 16

Train of Death

By seven o'clock the taxi had dropped us at a large grey barn. The driver bundled us out, assuring us it was the train station. I noticed a couple of blackboards with the times of the previous day's trains. To our surprise we found an information shed. It was closed. Two hours later the wooden shutter slid back revealing the employee. Very much in keeping with the Bolivian railway corporate image, the toothless old crone had considerable difficulty speaking. Eventually we interpreted her coca-stained gums enough to discover that the train to Brazil left the next day and we could only buy tickets on the day of departure.

True to her advice we returned at six o'clock the next morning. Already there were two huge queues. We didn't know which queue to join. Unfortunately the information department was still in bed and the blackboard operator was still mining his chalk. Much to my reluctance, we were forced to ask the locals which queue to join. Half a dozen started to talk at once, each with a different opinion. They eventually came to a consensus that the one they were in was the queue to Brazil. We thanked them and prepared ourselves for a long wait.

In the next three-and-a-half hours I noticed people swopping places in the queue ahead of us. Money was changing hands with each substitution. It was explained to me by my Bolivian neighbour that some of the people ahead were professional queuers. They would arrive at the station every day as early as two in the morning and start queueing. They would then wait there for up to eight hours and sell their place for the highest bid. I was told I could expect to pay the equivalent of up to three pounds for the best positions. I looked suitably impressed at this price because when telling such stories to foreigners the locals inevitably inflated the prices to shock us.

While he was explaining this I noticed three policemen with their heads together in conference. They nodded to each other as if they had come to a decision. They strode up to a young gringo, said a few words and marched him to a police car. They bundled him in and the car disappeared in a cloud of dust. His friend was left, staring in disbelief. Later, on the train, I discovered the police had arrested him on the pretext of being involved in black-market ticket trading. He had, like us, spent much of yesterday trying to get both information and tickets. The police had noticed he'd been there two days in a row and arrested him. He didn't make it back to join the train and I never discovered his fate.

At half-past nine the information shed opened. I thought it wise to check we were in the right queue. The locals sometimes deliberately told lies to foreigners. They saw it as a game to try to confuse us and waste our time. They didn't do this maliciously but they had a different idea of time to us and they imagined, if they had nothing to do, neither did we.

The old crone verified we were in the correct queue. At ten o'clock, they started selling the tickets; also the blackboard man arrived with his chalk and step ladder. The blackboard sign looked suspiciously confusing and so I asked the man in front of me if this was definitely the right queue for Brazil. He nodded and said he was sure that this was the right queue for Argentina. When I reminded him that four hours ago he had promised me that this was the right queue for Brazil, he gave me a confused shrug. He smiled with such righteous serenity that he would have made Mother Teresa look villainous.

We'd spent four hours in the wrong queue and now the correct one was about half a mile long. The locals who had been in on the joke from the beginning burst into riotous laughter at their joke. To show that I was not deflated I guffawed heartily and smacked the ring leader on the back. I congratulated them on their riotous prank; four hours in the wrong queue was a tremendous one-liner!

With my arm still around the chief jester, I whispered in his ear that when I returned from Brazil he and his family might suffer sudden and hideous deaths. I strode off to join the back of the other queue, with him staring worriedly after me. His chums, oblivious to his discomfort, were still chortling merrily and passing the joke on down the line, faster than we could walk.

After fifteen minutes the queue didn't seem to have moved, although many people were walking past clutching tickets. Leaving Dennis to keep the place, I went up to investigate and possibly buy a place further up. It was no wonder it wasn't moving. There was a team of about six people all dressed in black who were jumping in and out of the queue, buying three tickets at a time, flouting even the most basic rule of one ticket per person. The rest of the queuers stood and watched, unprepared to protest. The police made no effort to interrupt and carried on soaking up the early morning sunshine.

The men in black were the local mafia and according to one Bolivian, they have the police in their pockets. I could offer no contrary argument to explain the lack of police action. On a good day the mafia can buy up 80 per cent of the tickets and then resell them on the black market for up to twice their face value. The blatancy of the corruption made it almost farcical.

I walked back to Dennis and told him to go back to the vicarage to collect our bags. The train was leaving in just over an hour and I was determined to be on it.

I approached the mafia leader. He was very easy to identify. He was an extremely fat man of about twenty stones. Clothed in black shirt, opened almost to the waist, black trousers folded inside fancy leather black cowboy boots, he wore almost an entire jewellery shop in the form of gold rings, necklaces, bracelets and a big gold watch. He wore the customary gold-rimmed aviator sunglasses. I asked him for two tickets. The police noticed him talking to me so he led me off round the side of the station. The nominal price of the tickets was forty bolivianos which was about ten pounds. He asked for eighty bolivianos. Beads of sweat rolled down his face and he oozed grease and greed. I didn't lower myself to haggle and handed over the money with disdain. He made no indication that he noticed, and the money disappeared into sparkling, pudgy paws. Within seconds all traces of the transaction had disappeared as the notes were distributed for his assistants to mind. I was left clutching the tickets.

By the time Dennis arrived back at the station it was time to board. I was relieved to see the train was not steam but its rust and obvious antiquity did not instil confidence. We eventually worked out the complicated coach numbering and found our seats.

Apart from a mad woman lying across our seats, the carriages looked quite normal. There was a bench seating three facing a similar bench. No amount of coaxing would persuade the woman to leave and it was not until I prodded her that I convinced myself she was still alive. Eventually the other people on the coach determined to be seen helping the gringos started to swear at her extremely roughly. I prodded her again. She looked up at me like a bemused spaniel and rolled off the seat on to the floor. She lay there at my feet for quite some time until someone stood on her shoulder.

The train started to fill up. People stowed bags of rice, wheat, live chickens and even a small pig in every available space. In four feet of poorly padded bench, Dennis, a Bolivian and I squeezed. Opposite us sat a man and his small son, a woman and her medium-sized son, and a full-sized Bolivian. Between our benches were piled bags of rice. The temperature rose steadily as more people and sacks were crammed into the carriage. Little girls with buckets of homemade lemonade struggled through the crowds of people offering their refreshments.

The train shuddered and groaned readying to move off. The refreshment sellers pushed through to the doors and jumped off. One girl was caught between getting off the train or collecting the money from a sale. She chose to collect the money and the train moved away, leaving her stranded. She shrugged her young shoulders and carried on selling her cups of lemonade. She didn't seem too perturbed that the next scheduled stop was 1,500 kilometres away at the Brazilian border.

This train was one of the few land routes out of Bolivia and so any foreigners travelling through would tend to use it. Also it was rumoured to be one of the largest cocaine smuggling routes. In the eyes of the authorities, foreigners and cocaine were synonymous.

On this train there were seventeen foreigners and at least twenty plain-clothes policemen. The term plain-clothes is slightly misleading, as they made no pretence to merge into the background. They were instantly recognizable in their smart casual clothes and abundance of gold jewellery. They walked down the train in groups of three, their guns wedged between opulent flesh and designer trousers. As part of their unofficial uniform they wore dark sunglasses, usually with gold frames. They checked passports at random but they never missed the gringos. Dennis and I were smartly dressed, clean-shaven with short haircuts, as we'd been warned of possible drug planting. Apparently with a smart appearance we were less likely to look like disreputable travellers. Those backpackers who had been on the road for months were much more likely to suffer unwelcome police attention.

However, each new threesome checked our papers. The stamps in our passports identified that we were not just passing through and that we had been resident in Santa Cruz for quite a while. Dennis also had a Bolivian identity card pronouncing him to be a missionary. The policemen studied our papers thoroughly, asking us only perfunctory questions, to which we were able to reply in Spanish. By the time all the police had walked the length of the train we'd had our passports checked seven times. The intimidation had been considerable, but I started to relax as the last group passed through. They congregated at the back of the train.

We were barely two hours out of Santa Cruz and, with the relaxation of the police attention, the extreme physical discomfort of our cramped situation started to make its impression. I stretched out as far as the confining space would allow. I was just resigning myself to the discomfort when two policemen pushed through the throngs up the train. They disappeared into the next carriage. A few minutes later they returned with a nervous-looking foreigner in tow. They marched him down towards the end of the train.

After about ten minutes, they reappeared with the same foreigner, who looked shaken and very dishevelled. Minutes later they reappeared with another foreigner and the whole procedure started again. Over the next two hours they worked their way down the train. The time between collecting their next victim and reappearing in our carriage became less and less. Their systematic interrogation would soon be arriving at our carriage. I had no idea of what was happening in this interrogation but from the looks of the returning foreigners it was not pleasant. I sat waiting for my turn. The other passengers made no comment and I didn't dare look up as yet another gringo was led through our carriage. This was standard procedure for foreigners.

Apart from Dennis and me, there were two other foreigners in the carriage, a Brazilian and a Greek. The policemen came in and stood over the Greek. Very politely, they asked him to follow them. He bravely asked for what reason. They didn't answer but kindly lifted him to his feet and marched him down the train. This continuous intimidation was taking its toll. I sat with the fear at my powerless impotence turning to anger. The threat of unknown horrors had pushed me so far that I now welcomed their return, as at least a confrontation was preferable to the waiting. They returned the Greek to his seat and lifted the Brazilian to his feet. They dragged him off down the train.

I asked the Greek what had happened to him. They had taken him to the toilet at the end of the train and pushed him in. Inside the cramped space there were already three policemen, so his escorts waited outside the door. One policeman sat on the toilet seat while the other two crowded round him. He was pushed up against the wall and they stood inches from him, eyeing him. They had shouted 'Where is your cocaine?'

Before he had a chance to reply, the seated policeman had said 'It's probably up his ass.'

'Is it up your ass?' He had shaken his head.

'It's up his nose!'

They had then slammed him against the door and the policeman had forced back his head while the other stuck his fingers up his nose. Laughing, they had turned to their seated colleague and said, 'It is not up here.'

'It's in his belt.'

They opened his shirt and took off his moneybelt. They counted his money and helped themselves to a fifty-dollar bill. They smoothed him down and pushed him back out into the corridor. He had then been escorted back to his seat.

I asked him why he hadn't reacted to them. He told me that he knew of a German who had defied them a few months earlier. He had been taken in exactly the same circumstances but he'd told them that he had nothing for them. The policeman had reached into his own top pocket and produced a small bag of white powder. The German still said no and so the policeman, while looking into his eyes, had stuffed the bag into the German's top pocket. He was kept on the train and they returned him to Santa Cruz. He was put in jail and threatened with a twenty-year sentence. For two months he was not charged, but then he was given seventeen years. He had served a total of one month when his father paid some nameless authority a rumoured ten thousand dollars. He was allowed to leave the country.

When they marched the Brazilian past me, I desperately wanted to reach out for the gun tucked into the back of the policeman's trousers, stick the barrel up his nose and blow his head off. Their behaviour proved they were not interested in cocaine, just supplementing their incomes. I imagine if you were carrying cocaine, your contribution would be assessed accordingly. I was so incensed that I played out their deaths and my escape while waiting for their return. I knew there could be no escape, but at that moment so great was my fear that I seriously vowed to go down fighting.

The policemen escorted the Brazilian to his seat. They turned and without looking at us walked from the carriage. I couldn't sigh with relief as they might be back any minute. But after half an hour they had not returned. In their primitive devoutness, they feared the wrath of God and this had saved us. They believed Dennis and I to be missionaries, so they had left us alone. They didn't return to collect me. Their hypocrisy was sickening.

I have since been told by reliable sources that for the right price one can literally get away with murder. Later I met many of the other travellers and they reaffirmed their experiences. They had all been robbed of varying amounts, ranging from ten dollars. One English bloke on our train who had been carrying most of his money in notes was taken for five hundred dollars. They had not searched him, just taken out his belt and helped themselves. It gradually became clear that we were not going to be touched. My anger gave way again to physical discomfort. We had been going for about six hours and I had not been able to move. Suddenly the brakes screeched and locked and we came to a shuddering halt.

We had emerged from the jungle into a small clearing. A tiny village lay beside the tracks, its only purpose being to feed the bi-weekly train. The entire population ran alongside the carriages offering their foods.

Because of the crowding, passengers were unable to get to the doors. Instead they jumped from the windows and walked leisurely past the screaming locals to the edge of the jungle. Here they emptied their waterworks with uninhibited joy and then strolled back to the food stalls. The locals beckoned them, offering seats and displaying plates of food. They were conscious that in a few precious moments the source of their livelihood would again leave them to another four days of inactivity. They had to sell everything. Every member of the village was involved. They ran the length of the train with plates full of meat and rice for the people unprepared to leave the train. When they had sold their meals, they would rush back to their family stalls to get another plateful. The forest echoed with the prices of fresh lemonade, mangos, oranges and an assortment of meals. They ran around in a frenzy of activity, even the very young children were pressed into service, selling cigarettes and bubblegum.

The train hooted and everyone clambered back on board. The wheels groaned into action and we moved off. The villagers left their stalls and even old women ran alongside the departing train, intent on selling their last remaining meals. Eventually we left behind even the most persistent. I looked back along the rails to see them all standing staring after us, a lonely congregation of about one hundred, with their hands full of lemonade buckets and discarded plates. Motionless, they watched us disappear into the dusk as if we were their dearest relatives.

When night fell, out came the mosquitos. Since there was no light or ventilation on the train, the shutters were left open. The mosquitos whined around us as they seemed quite capable of keeping up with our chugging speed. A group of Bolivian men drank themselves into a noisy stupor and then collapsed in the aisles. It was impossible to move and with the temperature still in the eighties, I understood why it was called the train of death.

At one in the morning the little boy sitting opposite me decided he wanted to go to the toilet. Unable in the dark to move down the littered aisle I had to hold him up to the window. He happily pulled out his todger and pissed from the moving train. A considerable amount splashed from his unco-ordinated willy on to my legs. I was just grateful I was not among the passengers in the coaches behind. With their heads stuck out, they had been breathing in the cooler night air and had been sprayed instead. Their curses did nothing to dampen the little boy's flow.

At two a.m. we stopped again. This time there was no sign of a village but within seconds people appeared out of the jungle. They also carried plates of meat and rice and buckets of lemonade. There were no stalls visible but their food was warm. I found it baffling that at two in the morning in one of the most remote places in the world I was offered a cup of lemonade from a bucket. The train moved off again, leaving these railway caterers to their lonely lifestyle.

The rest of the trip proved uneventful but extremely uncomfortable. I didn't manage to get any sleep, although the Bolivians around me were snoring contentedly. I caught sight of some rheas just after dawn. They are the South American version of emus. The train startled them and they disappeared with a flurry of gangly legs. We eventually pulled up at the Bolivian border town of Quijaro. It had been a very tiring twenty-four hours.

CHAPTER 17

*

Brazil

We crossed the border into Brazil; leaving the dirt tracks of Bolivia to find paved highways. From adobe mud huts to brick and concrete buildings. But there was still the familiar inefficiency. Corumba, the border town, was still some way off. We pleaded with a very reticent taxi driver that perhaps he could earn more money driving his car than just polishing it.

He took us to a bus station where we joined a queue to have our passports stamped. On the brief drive, Corumba had not sparked any interest so we decided to keep moving. We caught a bus to Campo Grande through the Pantanal, a huge area of swamp land famed for its wildlife. Stretching from the road the scenery was flat and speckled with drainage ponds. The coach pulled up to a swollen brown river. The driver asked us to depart as he wasn't confident of his boarding technique. He drove safely on to the open ferry and we followed on foot.

The ferry set off down the piranha-infested river. Caymans basked on the steep sand banks. These members of the crocodile family rarely grow more than ten feet long. The ferry disturbed their sunbathing and, in the timeless tradition of the best Tarzan films, they slithered down the banks to disappear in the ripples. I scanned the water hopefully, searching for a scantily-dressed damsel to save from the jaws of these prehistoric monsters. Tarzan must have already been through as there were no distressed damsels visible. I contemplated pushing Dennis in, so that I could be a hero anyway. I decided against it, as I might be tempted to leave him splashing. The crocs surfaced briefly before swimming off to find seclusion.

Too soon we were back on board the coach speeding along a modern highway. From my elevated vantage point I spotted capybara. These are the world's largest rodents and they look like huge guinea-pigs. They stood in the shallows munching water lilies and staring blankly at herons fishing at the water's edge.

After a couple of days on the coach we arrived late one evening at Foz do Iguaçu. It is a very unremarkable town that has just grown up to service the visiting tourists.

The next morning we walked down the main street and found a taxi rank. The drivers didn't speak Spanish or English, only Brazilian Portuguese. Spanish and Portuguese are fairly similar and I found that if I spoke slowly they generally understood. The problem was that I couldn't understand their garbled replies.

With a very limited supply of language books available I often had to guess the translation of words. I had studied Latin and so I would choose an English word with an obvious Latin base and add an 'a'. I was surprised how often my guess at a Spanish word was correct. Other words I would translate simply by their context. This method often led to confusion. I guessed since Iguaçu was the name of the river, foz meant waterfall. Foz do Iguaçu: Waterfall of Iguaçu.

'*Cuánto costa ir a la foz?*'

He told us how much it would cost to the foz and it seemed reasonable. We climbed in and he drove off. We drove for about ten minutes until we came to a big bridge.

'That's a huge river. We must be pretty close to the falls.'

The taxi driver drove over and carried on along the road. We drove for another few minutes, without the slightest sign of the river. Dennis and I started to feel a touch apprehensive. I tried to communicate with the driver.

'*Dónde Foz?*'

He pointed up the road to the outskirts of a town.

'Dennis, the river is back that way. God know's where he is taking us.'

'Don't blaspheme, Oliver.'

'Sorry, Dennis.'

I turned back to the driver. We had now entered the outskirts of the town.

'*Dónde Foz?* Foz. Rio Grande. Aqua. Splosh. Foz.'

He stared at me dumbly. I demonstrated the action of a waterfall.

'Splosshh. Aqua. Foz.'

He pointed up towards the town.

'No! Rio. Aqua. Pssshh. Water.'

The driver stared out of his windscreen. I turned to Dennis. 'He's a stupid bastard.'

'Don't swear, Oliver.'

'Sorry, Dennis.'

We drove into the town and a sign welcomed us to Paraguay.

'Christ, we're in Paraguay. What the hell are we doing in Paraguay? There's just been a bloody coup in Paraguay. Shit!'

'Oliver, your language!'

'Sorry, Dennis.'

Dennis stated very calmly, 'We haven't even got our passports.'

'That's great. We're in Paraguay when everyone is being shot and we haven't even got our passports.'

I turned to the taxi driver and smiled. In English I said, 'What are we doing in Paraguay, you dog's dropping?' He just shrugged.

'Oliver!'

'Sorry, Dennis.'

I sat back in the seat and the driver pulled up to the pavement. Dennis leant out of the car window and beckoned a boy street-trader.

'*Chico, ven.*'

In Paraguay they speak Spanish and Dennis discovered this boy also spoke Portuguese. This town was called Foz and it was in Paraguay. Dennis explained we wanted to see the big river and he demonstrated the action of a waterfall. The boy replied,

'*Ah, las cataratas.*'

Cataratas meant waterfalls; not *foz* as we had presumed. He translated for us to the taxi driver. The falls were thirty kilometres in the other direction, back in Brazil. We thanked the boy and told the driver to take us back to our hotel in Brazil.

The bridge was the border and on the way back the police and army were searching the cars leaving the country. They seemed to be stopping every other car. We prayed they didn't stop us. Well Dennis prayed, I pretended.

We were pulled over. The policeman ordered our driver out by gesturing with the muzzle of his machine-gun. He opened the boot and stared at us through the back window. We looked up at him as serenely as we could. He waved us on.

Dennis smiled smugly, first at me and then up at the sky. We made it back to the hotel without further divine assistance.

Dennis's health finally collapsed, although he believed he was having a mental breakdown. He spent the day in bed, so I took the opportunity to indulge in chaperone-free entertainment. I went to an open-air restaurant where I met a beautiful Brazilian called Vera. She was a statuesque dental student from Rio de Janeiro. Unfortunately her parents arrived, so I arranged to meet her again the following evening.

Dennis was slightly happier and he told me he'd had a long talk with God.

'That's nice.'

God had told him to be strong and not to rely on me.

He realized that he was a burden and so he would go back to Santa Cruz. I nodded, although I was a little apprehensive at the prospect of travelling alone. I decided to book a hotel excursion to see the falls, as I was not prepared to risk the taxis.

The next morning Dennis stumbled out of bed to come with me. He looked awful. He'd had an allergic response to the hotel soap. However, he was determined to see the falls. The mini-bus stopped at another hotel to pick up a young couple. The woman was clearly Western, and this was confirmed when she spoke to her husband. 'You got the camera, Honey?'

'Yeah.'

Dennis's ears pricked up at the lilting intonation of Americanese. Before the couple had settled in their seats he asked,

'Hi, you guys American?'

'Yeah, sure, well my husband's Brazilian but we live in the States. What about you guys?'

Before Dennis could answer, I intervened, 'I'm English.'

Having cleared my name I sat back so they could talk apple pie.

'Yeah, I am. I'm Dennis and this is Oliver.'

'Hi, I'm Bonnie and this is Tulio.'

For the sake of this conversation, Oliver and Tulio had no choice but to be the strong silent types. A couple of kilometres later, Bonnie, with typical American reserve, commented, 'Dennis, you don't look that good.'

Dennis replied with equal modesty, 'No, I've had real bad diarrhoea.'

'Yeah? You taken any medication?'

'No, I've not been able to leave the bathroom long enough to find a drugstore. I'm running every five minutes. Aren't I, Oliver?'

I nodded non-committally, not wishing to be drawn in as character witness for Dennis's intestines.

Bonnie sighed sympathetically. She opened her handbag and took out a pill bottle.

'I was in the bathroom for two days, gushing from both ends, but these dried me up. They're real good. Take some.'

'Thanks.'

By the time we reached the falls they were chatting like old friends. There's nothing like flaccid bowels to bring people together. We walked down the path towards the huge river. As we turned a bend, through a break in the trees we had our first view of the waterfalls.

'Awesome!'

I had to agree. The Iguaçu falls are twenty metres higher than Niagara and twice as wide. The forest stretches away to the horizon like a saturated green sponge. It looked so verdant and overloaded with water that even the massive river seemed a minor tributary.

Thousands of gallons thundered over the sixty-metre precipice every second, creating plumes of steam. We stood at the base of the falls surrounded by spray and blazing rainbows. Above, spiralling in the thermals, flew the turkey vultures. We had come at the right time of year to see the falls at their most potent. As we stood, spellbound, a small brigade of coatimondis attacked my packed lunch. These forest dwellers look like long-tailed, skinny badgers.

Sadly we had to leave as Bonnie and Tulio had to catch a plane to São Paulo. We promised we could contact them if we ever got there.

That evening Dennis was feeling slightly better. He decided to come out with me but promised he wouldn't stay long as I had plans for Vera. He stayed all bloody evening. I couldn't work out whether he missed my 'three's a crowd' hints out of naïvete or if it was a cunning plot to save me from sin. Whatever, it failed, as Vera gave me a kiss and said that I could come to her hotel at twelve-thirty. 'Yippee,' I thought, doing a couple of stretches. I arrived at the appointed time after a quick bath. She was sitting in the foyer with her parents. Although I couldn't see a wedding ring, I beat a hasty retreat before I was spotted.

I returned disappointed to the hotel. Dennis was still praying. We decided to fly to São Paulo so that Dennis could return to Santa Cruz. He had decided, in his illness, that he could not cope with the rigours of the trip.

At Igaçu's unbuilt airport we bumped into Vera and her parents. They gave me their address and I shuddered at the horrific eligibility that being a foreigner created. With my fingers crossed behind my back, I promised to phone when I got to Rio de Janeiro. By the time we arrived in Rio the diarrhoea pills were starting to take effect, and Dennis, in an improved state of health, decided to stay a few more days.

We booked a hotel with a swimming pool from the airport information desk. Not only did it look luxurious in the brochure but it was convenient to the central bus station. On the drive to the centre, São Paulo looked just another concrete sprawl. It was grey, wet and very uninviting. After an hour driving along the modern highways through the concrete blocks we still hadn't arrived at the centre. I started to understand what it is about São Paulo that makes it special. It's huge. The official population is just over ten million, but the four satellite squatter towns merged to the boundaries make the actual figure closer to fourteen million.

Dennis spotted a McDonald's from the airport bus and, as the hotel pool proved to be a large leaf-filled bucket, we went out to commiserate over a burger. I disagreed on principle but, faced with the opportunity of junk food for the first time in five months, my resolve broke. It was the happiest I had seen Dennis in ages as he tucked into his burger, strawberry shake and large fries.

It was reasonably late as we strolled in the warm evening

back to our hotel. We were both very tired but, even so, my eyes followed the shapely legs of a beautiful black girl. As she walked towards us dressed in a stunning blue leather mini-skirt and low-cut jacket, I was momentarily frozen. Drawing closer she parted scrumptious red lips provocatively. As my eyes dropped to check out her other assets, I noticed something wasn't quite right. It wasn't until she had passed that I realized what it was. She had an adam's apple. She was a man. It was a good job I was shy!

The next day we contacted Bonnie and Tulio. After a quick update on Dennis's bowel movements, they took us around a craft fair in the main square, Praça da Republica. Under the oak-tree-sized rubber plants there were stalls selling everything from fossils to fresh pineapple. I bought a dollar bracelet for one of my sisters.

We had a drink at the top of the Edifício de Italia (São Paulo's tallest building). From the viewing gallery we looked out at a sea of concrete skyscrapers. In every direction the high-rise buildings faded away to merge into the grey sky. São Paulo is built on an almost flat plateau. The buildings, viewed from the pinnacle of the tallest skyscraper, seem to have levelled any natural hills. It left the impression of a round, flat, gently rippling lake. Standing at the very hub of this huge concrete millpond, it was hard to believe there were millions of Paulistinos (inhabitants of São Paulo) living and working underneath it.

Arriving back late I realized the hotel was set in one of the world's most blatant red-light districts. There were prostitutes everywhere, wearing little more than goose pimples. There were also six-foot-four transvestites in short skirts, their shoulders bulging from their plunging necklines. Dennis, who hadn't been to private school, was amazed. From behind the safety of the hotel's ten-foot security gates he snapped away happily with his camera.

The next morning we went for a trip on the underground, which has only two lines, north-south and east-west. We went on both, riding to the end of the line. It was the cleanest and most modern tube I have ever been on. Picking a station at random, we came up to discover a supermarket. Inside there were several small shops and I found a boutique for women's clothes. I had been given some large hints that Anita wanted a bikini. I pretended not to notice the hints until they reached the 'It's such a sunny day I wish I had a bikini. What are you going to buy me in Brazil?' level of subtlety.

The shop assistant asked, 'Can I help you, sir?'

Slightly embarrassed I replied, 'Erm, no. I'm just looking.'

I searched the shop until I found a rack of bikinis and selected a colour. Then it struck me, which size? I had no idea, but I thought logically and cupped my hands to resemble a breast. Unfortunately with both hands occupied in bosom role-play I couldn't stretch the bikini top over them, to see if it fitted. I couldn't ask Dennis as he had taken refuge at a discreet distance. I think he believed any connection with women's underwear would seriously endanger his chance of being ordained.

I tried to hold the bikini top in place with my teeth, but by now the shop assistant was eyeing me suspiciously. Worried I might be arrested, I smiled at her and removed the black and silver bikini top from between my teeth. I selected 'small'; at least it would be pleasantly revealing. I also grabbed a little cocktail dress. I paid and ran from the shop.

Outside, I sighed my relief. Shopping for women's clothes while trying to remember the size and position of all their bumpy, wobbly bits was very taxing. Give me a hideously poisonous coral snake any day! I went for a drink; Dennis went to church.

Early the next morning Bonnie and Tulio took us for a trip down to the local seaside resort, Santos. We passed one of the four shanty towns, or *favelas*. These towns don't have names as they don't officially exist. They are just known as A, B, C and D. Tulio explained that most Brazilian people were very resentful of the *favelas'* inhabitants. He said that many stayed there to avoid paying taxes. He pointed out huts with cars outside and television aerials poking from the corrugated roofs. I asked whether they had running water and sanitation. They didn't, but they were still seen as free-loaders.

The population of Brazil is 135 million and the industrialized south-east contains a fifth of the total population. São Paulo is one of the fastest-growing cities in the world. It already covers over 1,500 square kilometres. Brazil's urban population is growing at over twice the national average. This is putting huge pressures on the city's services.

We drove past the boundaries of São Paulo into the mountains. The road down to the coast was staggering. It was bridge and then tunnel as it meandered and burrowed through the mountains. Unfortunately it was impossible to stop as the road was full of blaring juggernauts. They ply constantly, day and night, between Santos and São Paulo. Santos is Brazil's biggest port, handling over forty per cent of its imports and over half of its exports.

Each new view of the Valley of Death was spectacular. It is so attractively named because the chemical factories on the coast have made the area one of the most polluted in the world. However, we spent a great day lying on the beach and eating corn ice-cream.

By now Dennis felt totally recovered, and prepared to go on. We said goodbye to Bonnie and Tulio and set off for Rio de Janeiro.

CHAPTER 18

*

Amethyst

As the coach drove down from the mountains on the approach to Rio, the road was lined with theme motels. These buildings were modelled on castles, ships and other bizarre notions. The motels outside Santa Cruz were renowned as brothels. I wondered whether these were also brothels and, if they were, would the employees wear costumes relevant to the theme? Whatever the answer, I seriously questioned the motivations of anyone who built a papier-mâché castle motel. In my new role of missionary-aide, perhaps I should have tried to save them.

We found a hotel close to Copacabana beach and booked an excursion to see Concordia, the huge Christ statue over-looking the city. The bus couldn't make it up the last stretch of the steep mountain road. As we departed from the bus to board taxis, someone took our photographs. We spent forty minutes at the statue looking at the incredible views of Rio de Janeiro. I had a hard time as Dennis came over all religious and it started to rain. He kept crossing himself and mumbling. I eventually persuaded him to leave the statue and head back to the taxi. However, we had only descended one flight of steps when Dennis was captured by a cunningly positioned souvenir shop. He was now overcome with another ingrained tradition – tourist junk buying. It proved even harder to get him away from the plaster models of Concordia. I only managed to prise him away by replying to his comments as he picked another plastic eyesore.

'Um, this is lovely.'

'No, Dennis it's crap, and the price is blatant robbery.'

I believe Americans are second only to the Japanese when it comes to souveniritis. I had to raise my voice considerably and offer my opinion on all the items before Dennis started to become embarrassed.

'Ssh Oliver! These people can speak English.'

'Of course they can. They can con a sucker at twenty paces.' This finally did the trick and he led me back to the taxi.

At the bus the photographer had amazingly developed the pictures and imprinted them on to a plate. As we re-boarded he offered them for sale. Most of the Americans were delighted with the porcelain snapshots.

On the journey to the hotel the tour guide explained over the bus tannoy that we would soon be going through an area where on one side of the road were very rich people's houses and on the other poor people lived. She explained in her pidgin English that we would stop so that we could take 'phots'. The bus did stop and I was amazed to see the tourists jump off to take pictures of 'poor people'.

The tour guide pointed out one child who didn't have any shoes. As they whirred away with their thousand-dollar cine cameras, I understood why Rio de Janeiro has one of the world's highest murder rates. However, the slums seemed positively palatial compared with Bolivian squalor.

I was constantly oppressed by Rio. It wasn't the paradise I had imagined. It was the unpleasant proximity of two extremes. The tour guide told us a beach-side apartment would cost more than one million dollars. Walking down these opulent roads you could suddenly find yourself amid horrendous poverty. At least in Bolivia the poverty was fairly uniform, so you could adjust to it. The unequal distribution of wealth here was sickening.

The government announced drastic plans to curb the hyper-inflation. They fixed the exchange-rate at one dollar to one new cruzado. The Brazilian bank notes were baffling. In circulation, there were four editions of notes. Firstly there were cruzaros, then new cruzeros, then cruzados and now they printed new cruzados. Each new edition of notes would effectively knock on an extra three zeros. One new cruzado was worth one thousand old cruzados, and one hundred thousand new cruzeros. It was extremely complicated even by South American standards. I decided on a method that anything with more than six zeros was practically worthless. With this harsh exchange rate our dollars were now considerably reduced in value. We had planned to stay for the Carnival, but we decided with the inflated prices we couldn't afford it.

We were returned to our hotel by the tour bus and we decided to go to the Sugar Loaf Mountain.

The Pão de Açúcar is on the edge of the harbour. You need to get two cable cars to scale the top. It was now late and we watched the sunset from the summit of this huge rock. Looking down, Rio appeared the most beautiful city in the world. It is built between and around grey hump-backed mountains. Its boundaries are marked by five curved beaches facing out to the island-freckled Guanabara Bay. A huge mountain range isolates Rio from the dark interior, forcing it to sit like an island on the edge of this huge continent.

Darkness fell and the dusk obscured all thoughts of poverty. Instead a magical tapestry of lights punctured by the mountain humps unravelled beneath us. An enormous spotlight lit up the custodian statue of Christ on a distant peak, and the beaches were marked out with all-year fairy lights.

Brazilians boast, 'God made the world in six days; the seventh he devoted to Rio.' It was certainly spectacular.

Everyone started to make their way back to the cable car. As I stood looking across the Atlantic towards England, I noticed purple thunder clouds racing in, lightning dancing between them. Seconds later they were overhead, the rain pelting down.

The last crowd of sightseers ran for cover and packed into the cable car bay. Thunder raged and lightning exploded around us with such brutal force it was decided to halt the car until the storm had passed.

The lightning struck the cable and sizzled up towards us. The lights went out and left us in the dark standing in an inch of rainwater. After fifteen minutes they managed to get a back-up generator working and the lights came on. The nervous cheering had just died down when another massive bolt smashed into the line. This time the lights blew for good. We waited for over an hour as the lightning burned up the night.

A party of American evangelical tourists decided to raise our spirits by singing 'We will overcome'. The storm was unable to compete and rumbled away across the bay.

I managed to push forward for the second cable-car trip down. Most of the evangelical party were also with me.

'Ah, gee, were you scared, Mary?'

'Heck no, if the Lord wants me to die, I'll die.'

I thought this was a particularly selfish thing to say because if Mary had done something so bad that the Lord wanted her to die, I would have been sacrificed into the bargain. I was very glad when we reached terra firma and away from the harikari Christian sisterhood. We made it back to our hotel and decided to spend another day in Rio. I did after all need to check out the bodies on Copacabana beach.

Early the next morning we went in search of some suntan oil. I found a chemist, selected a bottle with factor four written across the chest of a busty blonde and took it to the counter. The two men and a woman serving looked at me in that 'We were having a nice chat until you came in,' shopkeeper way. They didn't move to take my oil so I eventually waved it in front of the woman. As luck would have it she was the start of the purchasing procedure. She ripped the bottle from my grasp and hand wrote me a double receipt. She gave me the receipts and gestured for me to move on down the line. I shuffled to the next man. He took my money and my recently won receipts. He tore one receipt off and returned the other. He then ushered me to move again down the line. They were clearly into job sharing in a big way.

I moved to the final man, clutching my one remaining memento of the transaction. There had been no sign of my suntan oil since the treadmill had started. The third man held out his hand for my receipt. I gave it up with a slight protest. He miraculously revealed a wrapped bottle of suntan oil. I felt like asking for a receipt, but I decided my Portuguese couldn't cope with the baffling complexity of their procedure.

The beach was also a disappointment. I'd expected to check out some serious sex goddesses; instead the water was brown and cold and the sand was packed with beached whales. I'd had enough of Rio.

The next morning we left for the bus station. The bus to Montevideo didn't leave for five hours. Dennis had spotted an advertisement in the hotel magazine for a jeweller's so we set off to fill in time. Brazil is famed for its cheap amethysts and he wanted to buy some.

We arrived at an impressive stone building and walked into the marble foyer. The man behind the desk said that unfortunately the jewel factory was just closing so we couldn't have a guided tour to see the polishing of the stones. The shop, however, was still open. We had to sign our names in the visitor's book. A uniformed young lady escorted us up in a highly polished brass lift.

The doors slid back and a man wearing a dinner-jacket and holding a clipboard welcomed us by name. There were cut-glass chandeliers everywhere and the walls were covered in glass cases, with carefully arranged million-dollar jewellery. Our dinner-jacket man introduced us to Clara, who would help us view whatever we liked. This elegant woman led us to her desk and sat us down. I felt very underdressed in my jeans and T-shirt. She sat opposite us, modelling a chic little number from Paris. She asked if we would like something to drink. I ordered a Black Russian but settled for a coke. Standing behind her was a trainee model who went to fetch our drinks. There were only about five other customers, each sitting at their own desks served by former winners of the Miss Brazil beauty competition.

While waiting, our hostess made highly trained small talk. Our cokes returned and Clara lit my cigarette. She asked what we wanted to see. After a sophisticated pause I replied we were interested in amethysts. The trainee was a bit slow with the ashtray so I dropped the ash into the shagpile. She quickly put one in front of me and apologized for the delay. I told her not to worry.

Our hostess asked what price range we would like to view. I suggested that although these were very much minor presents, we may want up to one hundred dollars. She sent the server to find something in that price range. The trainee returned with two dusty drawers. They were unused to dealing in anything under one thousand dollars.

Dennis studied the jewels and decided he couldn't afford anything. I was horrified. After all this time we had to buy something. I decided that I might as well buy an amethyst for my mother. I chose the cheapest jewel they had, which was still sixty dollars. The amethyst was in a gold setting and Clara complimented my excellent taste. She wrote a beautiful scrolled receipt and sealed it in a gold envelope. The jewel disappeared into the depths of a velvet drawbag. She thanked us for our custom and made us promise the next time we were in Rio we would drop in. We joined the uniformed elevator boy for the long trip to the ground floor. We were given a complimentary lift to the bus station and caught a bus to Montevideo.

I've since had a postcard from them, addressed to a most valued customer. They look forward to my next visit.

Thirty-six hours later we crossed the border at Chuy

into Uruguay. Early in the morning we passed through the seaside resort of Punta del Este, one of the stops on the round-the-world yacht race. It seemed amazingly clean and wealthy, and as we drove down the coast road the revelations continued. The woods were pine and eucalyptus. But the staggering thing was the holiday homes. The coast road was lined with affluent villas in a variety of styles. There were Swiss-style cabins, and I even noticed an English thatched cottage, complete with roses. Parked in the drives of these villas were cars of the nineteen thirties, forties and fifties.

Although it was still early morning I could see Uruguay had a cobweb staleness. Everything about it spoke of decaying prosperity. Uruguay was sagging at the corners and wrinkling fast.

We drove on into the outskirts of Montevideo. Not only were its buildings, cars and economy middle aged, its people seemed to average about forty. It could have been the film set of *Chitty-Chitty-Bang-Bang*. As a strong believer in 'keep the under-tens in damp caves beneath castles' policy, I decided I was going to like Montevideo.

We found a tourist information office right beside the bus station and were given the name of a decent hotel convenient to the town centre. We booked in and went to bed.

We got up at eleven and went to explore. We needed to get visas from the Argentine Embassy and eventually spotted the blue and white flag. I collected a form which demanded more detail than the Magna Carta and was instructed to go the Argentine bank and pay the visa fee directly into a numbered account. It all seemed very dodgy, but I returned with the receipt and handed it over with my passport for the appropriate stamp. We were told to return the next day to collect them.

We went off to sample the town, and as Montevideo is famed for its beef, we found a cheap grill restaurant. I picked out my own chunk of steak and they then grilled it on an amazingly hot and smoky grate at the front of the shop.

The next day we queued patiently in the Argentine Embassy. Dennis collected his passport but I had to wait a further three hours. They clearly had not forgotten the Falklands.

Officially equipped, we decided to go back along the coast to the resort, La Floresta. We spent a few days on the beach watching the vintage cars. I desperately wanted to introduce Dennis to sin but I couldn't even find any for me. All this travelling, however, was putting pressure on his praying time. He had missed Mass two Sundays in a row. I told him that, come Judgement Day, two black marks in God's attendance book might weigh heavily against him. He said he would pray for me.

CHAPTER 19

*

Bribe

Dennis and I sat at a roadside café in the warm Montevideo evening. While I moistened my throat with six beers, he sucked fizzy pop through a straw. We both liked the atmosphere which was calm and relaxed. There wasn't the aggressive, speculative power of Brazil. The city had the dignity and elegance of an old man who has just bought his last pair of slippers.

Recently the economy has stabilized after years of hyper-inflation. Money from the disastrous Argentine economy had been siphoned into the Uruguayan banks. This money has moisturized the tired lines and hinted at rejuvenation.

We handed our passports to the bus driver as we boarded, so that he could have them stamped when we crossed into Argentina at midnight. I was sad to leave Montevideo. I felt that if I ever had a chance to come back it wouldn't be the same. The old man would either have drifted into eternal sleep and his slippers found their way to Oxfam, or would be sporting a blond wig and cowboy boots.

I woke up as we crossed at Fray Bentos on the border. This had been an ambition of mine for a long time. I had grown up on Fray Bentos steak and kidney pies, and now I had Fray Bentos stamped for eternity in my passport.

Anyone who grew up with working parents will be familiar with these tinned pies. They are always the last thing left in the cupboard for emergencies when your parents are away. They take considerable skill to open and then they rise miraculously in the oven. You eat the layers of crispy pastry and thick gravy and throw away the unrecognizable lumps masquerading as meat. Despite their general unpleasantness, they are always remembered fondly. I expect it is because after a week of teenage self-catering, beer and cornflakes, a Fray Bentos was my only venture into following parental advice, 'Make sure you eat properly!'

We drove for the first time on to Argentine soil. A twenty-foot sign welcomed us, '*Las Malvinas son de Argentina.*'

After the Second World War, Argentina was the world's seventh richest country. Now, after forty years of corruption, coups and dictatorship, it is poorer on paper than Bolivia. However, Argentina still has wealth. Or rather individuals have great fortunes. They just don't keep them in Argentina.

In Buenos Aires, the newspapers told of the latest bout of political unrest. Twenty-four people had been killed in a bomb attack. We decided to move on to Córdoba.

Fourteen hours later we booked into a nine-dollar hotel next to the bus station. The walls were so thin we could hear the departure announcements. Dennis went looking for spiritual refreshment; I had mine with ice.

It now seemed as if we were just travelling from bus station to bus station. After almost a month of the road we wanted to get somewhere we could relax. We decided to head straight back to Santa Cruz instead of going to Chile.

At every bus departure we greatly envied our fellow travellers who had family to wave them off. Departing Córdoba, we sought comfort by adopting a surrogate family of wavers. Much to their confusion, we gestured our fond farewells to them through the coach window.

We arrived at Guemes and then caught the connection to Poçitos on the Argentine border. With each town that brought us closer to Bolivia, there was a tangible decline in wealth. I felt we were burrowing to the rotted core of South America. For me, Bolivia symbolized South America's problems – transitory wealth, looted and squandered by tinpot generals. It had started in 1561 with the Spanish and is continuing today.

At Poçitos we met two Belgian girls who were touring. These were the only other foreigners we had seen for a long time. We got chatting to them and discovered they were nurses heading for Ecuador on their way back to Belgium. They were also going to catch the train to Santa Cruz. The train left on the Bolivian side of the border.

At the immigration post we were told that they only had one *salida* stamp, and it was at the Argentine train station back down the road. We eyed the official dubiously and went to find the station. We had to join a long queue as passengers off the one through train were waiting to enter Bolivia. We were unable to buy tickets for this train as it fills up in Buenos Aires and the passengers live on the train for three days.

I handed my passport to one of the two seated policemen for a *salida*. He looked long and hard at the stamps. He held it up accusingly, 'You haven't got an *entrada*.'

I took my passport and checked. True enough, when we had crossed into Argentina the bus driver had got a *salida* from Uruguay but he had not got an *entrada*.

This may seem a simple thing to check, but my passport had about thirty stamps in it and emigration officials never stamp on the next available space. We were not officially in the country.

'You will have to go back to where you came in and get an *entrada*!' He looked suspiciously like ex-president Galtieri.

'But that is two thousand kilometres away.' He waved me aside and held out his hand for Dennis's passport. I stood my ground.

'We're together.'

The official looked up at me. 'I not sure if there is

anything I can do.' He held my stare and the silence clarified his message. He wanted a bribe. Scared stiff, I slipped a twenty-dollar bill in the passport and, gesturing at Dennis, I said, 'We have the same problem.' I offered my passport back to him. He needed no prompting and took it from me. He leaned back and opened the passport so the note slid on to his lap under the table The note evaporated and he stamped my passport.

He took Dennis's passport and stamped it, laughing, 'No problems for an American!'

When we were outside Dennis sighed his relief and said, 'Did you hear that? "No problems for an American!" You were lucky.'

'Yes, Dennis.' My heart was still thumping horribly and I couldn't cope with his naïveté. I had to walk away before I upset his delicate morality and nationalist delusions by telling him the truth.

We waited for the Belgians and walked over the bridge into Bolivia. We were immediately back among the stifling poverty. The little border town is called Yacuiba and is a poor but bustling place. We managed to change some dollars and we were surrounded by children begging for coins and men with wheelbarrows offering to carry our bags. Women jostled us with trays trying to sell us cigarettes and chewing-gum. There was just one street that led from the border bridge to the train station.

Halfway along the muddy track was the Bolivian immigration shed. The official welcomed us warmly and charged us a five-dollar fee for our *entrada*. I wasn't aware that there was such a fee, but paying officials was now second nature.

We walked up to the train station, surrounded by children. The ticket office was shut and we discovered that all the tickets for today's train had been sold. The locals crowded around us with their tickets. This was no organized black market. A timid little man said how much he wanted and we said how much we would pay. We then exchanged money for tickets. All the local children crowded around us, watching with open mouths at this wheeling and dealing. The train was not leaving for two hours, so we decided to go for some food with the two Belgians.

We sat under a tree at the only table at the only café in Yacuiba. We ordered chicken and rice. Typically, the chicken was tough as nails. The emaciated, mange-ridden dogs grovelled for our scraps.

The more dominant of the Belgians stuck out her chin and said, 'We're what you would call friends.'

We sat in silence at this revelation. It took a surprisingly long time for me to fathom it out. It was completely out of the blue and I didn't consider sexual preference a topic for conversation over lunch, especially with strangers. The silence was becoming awkward, and I was praying Dennis wouldn't say 'I hope we can all be friends.'

I replied, 'We are what you call "just" friends.'

They laughed, and thankfully Dennis then caught on as I didn't fancy explaining the concept of homosexuality. His face lit up. Talking to lesbians was yet another new experience.

The poverty in Yacuiba was perhaps the worst I saw in South America. A woman walked past us with her baby under her arm. Its head was out of proportion to the rest of its tiny body. It hung to one side, its neck unable to support the weight.

'Malnutrition. It will be dead within a week.'

I became irrationally cross that the Belgians were giving their chicken bones to the dogs. They were so matter-of-fact about their malnutrition diagnosis, but meanwhile kept cooing about the poor dogs. I couldn't blame them, as they'd probably dealt with so much human death and suffering that they'd become hardened.

We bought some biscuits and apples for the journey and found our seats. The train had filled quickly and there was no room to stow our bags. There were boxes above our seats and so I asked to whom they belonged. A little man sitting on the other side of the aisle said they were his. When I said we wanted to stow our bags there, he jumped up and made room for them and even put them up for us.

Apart from the two Belgians, I didn't spot any other gringos or policemen. No one wanted to smuggle cocaine into Bolivia.

The journey was even more uncomfortable than the Train of Death. The carriages were so packed with boxes and sacks that we couldn't move an inch.

Although the poorest South American country, Bolivia is also the most expensive for general commodities. Therefore a few enterprising peasants shop for products in Argentina and Brazil and bring the goods back to Bolivia. The authorities have tried to curb this trade by placing baggage restrictions on train passengers.

The ticket collector and two other officials entered our carriage and started to ask to whom various bags belonged. The little man sitting across the aisle soon completed his baggage quota. The officials found bags under seats and under blankets on the seats. The little man made his young daughter lie on top of a pile of boxes and pretend she was deaf and dumb. The officials found more boxes stowed away, and when they asked who they belonged to, no one owned up. Any bag not claimed is automatically confiscated.

They made to lift it. The little man jumped up and said it was his. The officials frowned and moved on again to another box which no one had claimed. Under pressure the little man owned up again. He guaranteed that this was his last box. Unfortunately in the very next row was another of his boxes, which he'd forgotten about. But this really was his last – except for three sacks and a couple more boxes. He sent his young friend to the next carriage to claim further parcels. When the officials had finally passed through, the little man with his careful distribution had minimized his fine.

As we started to approach Santa Cruz, he sent his family to collect his boxes. They went off in each direction and staggered back, weighed down with parcels. He had cleverly selected the last row of seats in the carriage. They used the extra room to pile their goodies between the seat and the wall. They kept disappearing down the carriages and bringing back more boxes. They heaped them together until they were right up to the train roof. They then collected more and sat on them in the aisle.

The train stopped at a station. There had never been a schedule, so I imagined it was Santa Cruz. They may have had the technology to instal a tannoy system, but they certainly didn't have the inclination. Before the train had come to a complete halt, the little man's friend had jumped out of the window and screamed for a taxi. The little man then started throwing his boxes out of the window as his wife and daughter passed them to him. The friend was catching them from the window and cramming them into the taxi. The train hooted and started to pull away but the family kept throwing. I looked out of the window and the scene was being repeated by similar groups all down the train.

Finally the train picked up speed and the family briefly collapsed into their seats. Amazingly they had unloaded almost all their boxes. They only stayed seated for a couple of minutes. They then disappeared back down the train and started to bring back more boxes, bottles of cooking oil, tins of beef and sacks of pasta. They managed to completely re-fill their seats with packages. We finally pulled into Santa Cruz station and left them to their frantic unloading.

Back in the Santa Cruz priest's house we collapsed. We were glad to be back, but it had been fun. We had made our impressions on each other, most noticeably in our language. I cursed considerably less than before and Dennis now swore like a part-time trooper.

*

CHAPTER 20

Carnival

We arrived back in Buena Vista in time for the carnival. Anita took me back to her bosom, and I was surprised to see how much I'd missed her. After all the trouble with the bikini, it was too small. She gave it to Charo. However, she was very happy with her dress.

Despite her presents she still kept running away from me. I consider new tactics. Somebody very old once sang, 'Money can't buy love.' I wondered whether this applied to traveller's cheques.

The carnival dragged Buena Vista from rural slumber to bustling metropolis. Everyone cleaned out store cupboards and offered them for rent. Most people could stay with relatives. The enterprising locals living on the plaza were determined to make some money out of this influx of people. They put tables and chairs outside their homes and sold cheap meals of meat and rice.

All the organization had started while I had been away. Everyone was conscripted into party groups called *cumparsas*. Each *cumparsa* had its own colours. Money was collected from the *cumparsa* members and rolls of cheap material bought in Santa Cruz. They then made shirts for their members. The scraps of material were not wasted, they were made into wrist and head bands.

Guy and I were invited to join the trendy young people's *cumparsa* which was called *Huacha* (Little Calf). Our team colour was a rather putrid green. Unfortunately I'd arrived too late to get a customized shirt. Charo lent me a green T-shirt. Anita completed the uniform by tying a green sash round my forehead and lengths of material round my wrists. We practised our *cumparsa* chant, 'Which *cumparsa* is best? *Bomba Huacha!*'

Charo, Anita and I prepared some water bombs. We filled balloons with water and went looking for victims. There were continual waterfights with other *cumparsas* and even among ourselves, so one had to be prepared. Unfortunately there were no suitable targets, so I emptied my balloons down the unsuspecting necks of Charo and Anita and prevailed upon the sanctity of the priest's house before they recovered.

Every night of the week one of the *cumparsas* hosted a party in the arena. All the other *cumparsas* would be invited. We all sat around the main dance floor in our tribal groups. At the end of the evening the host *cumparsa* would crown its *cumparsa* queen.

Huacha party night was the liveliest, and it was the first chance I had had to see our *cumparsa* queen. She was very beautiful, but she didn't have Anita's appeal. She'd been born in Buena Vista, but now lived in Santa Cruz.

Friday night was the crowning of the carnival queen. Every *cumparsa* was represented and the square was bright with gaudy colours. The two young runners-up were presented with flowers, and much to *Huacha*'s delight, our queen was chosen as this year's carnival queen. She stood on the stage in a stunning, flowing gold dress. It was pleated and trimmed with white lace which contrasted with her bronzed skin. She shone with beauty and elegance as her crown was rested by the mayor on her ringletted, glossy hair. With flowers clasped to her breast, a single tear ran from her large hazel eyes. She transcended eroticism and was simply the greatest picture of serene beauty I'd ever seen.

Brushing the tear from her cheek, she smiled, her lips parting to reveal rotted and discoloured teeth. Like many

South Americans, she had fallen foul of television advertising and had spent her youth drinking cola. With no dental health care available, her perfection had been ruined by a transitory Western fashion. I saw her in that one brief moment totally encapsulating the state of South America. She was beauty, innocence, purity and infinite potential, disfigured and corruped by Western greed and abuse. I kissed Anita and left for the Whitehouse.

In the Whitehouse garden we had several cocoa trees. The fruit was an eight-inch orange pod that grew straight off the tree's trunk and branches. Inside the pod were the seeds that are dried to make cocoa and eventually chocolate. The seeds are padded in the pods with a white, jelly sap. This sap is very succulent and is considered by the locals to have aphrodisiac qualities.

Midday Saturday, I struggled up to Anita's house, ladened down with armfuls of chocolate pods. My courting had been stretched to a new level of initiative. Anita was no longer a project to test my resourcefulness. This was a crusade, a mission, a necessity. If this latest effort failed, I would have to borrow the cleaner's wheelbarrow and carry up the entire chocolate tree. Outside her house workmen were still putting the final touches to the plaza decorations.

On the last three days of the carnival the plaza was filled with thatched promenades. There was a hive of activity as a large stockade was built for the bullfighting. Stalls were set up with the usual fete games. There was dart-throwing at playing cards on a board. Also an airgun shooting range, the barrels so bent that accuracy was actually a disadvantage.

There were even bunco booths: extremely unskilful card tricksters with the requisite three cards. You were challenged to follow the queen. Considering the constant threat of poverty, I expected to see a great display of sleight of hand. Mug after mug followed the queen to its resting position and then reached for his money to state the position. Meanwhile the trickster would swop the cards.

I watched a couple of more streetwise youths who came with their money already in their hands. In these circumstances the trickster employed the services of his entourage of friends. These men posing as members of the public would accidentally stumble in front of the contestant or tap him on the shoulder. The trickster would take advantage of this diversion and swop the cards. The most incredible thing about the whole charade was the look of total disbelief from the contestants when they guessed wrongly.

The Bolivians have adopted these Western fete games as many of their own were frowned upon. They recently stopped holding their version of blind man's buff. The game consisted of burying a duck up to its neck in the sand. The competing children would be blindfolded and given a stick. The first child to knock the duck's head would be given his very own duckling.

The day was still very warm so I went off in search of peace and refreshment. I found Dennis in the priest's house. Together we strolled over to watch the bullfighting. People had already started to crowd round the stockade. The more agile sat on the top pole.

Anita had saved me a place, and no sooner had I made myself comfortable than a truck arrived and dumped a severely trussed bull. It lay on the ground, so well bound it was unable to move. The crowd cheered as it was kicked by one of the organizers. Two others joined in until blood was flowing freely from its nose. They then untied it. The beast staggered to its feet and, being a highly trained field biologist, I noticed it was in fact a cow. Apparently with this breed the cows are almost as aggressive. However, I imagined that anything would become aggressive after having been kicked in the nose for a couple of minutes.

The young men of the village stood huddled together

inside the stockade. They were encouraged by the crowd to take on the cow. The houses of the plaza made up one side of the stockade and so they stood in the doorways, ready to disappear if danger threatened. The more foolhardy started to taunt the cow by walking out a few metres and jeering at it. They also lobbed stones at it. Despite the crowd's jeers, however, they never strayed far from their bolt holes.

One youth climbed into the stockade and staggered up to the cow. His courage was clearly alcoholic. The crowd cheered as he beckoned the cow to him. The cow needed no encouragement as it saw the chance of rightful retribution for one of its tormentors. It pawed the dust and charged. For a second the youth stood his ground, intent on a sidestep. However, his resolve cracked and instinct took over. He turned and ran with his arms spread heavenwards, imploring for longer, faster legs. He was unanswered and within three strides was overtaken and disappeared under a flail of hooves and dust.

The cow, in its eagerness for vengeance, had charged too hard and its impetus carried it on over the crumpled figure. It stumbled on, just regaining control before the wall loomed.

The crowd gasped disappointedly as the youth rose to his feet. He was also amazed that he could stand and that he was miraculously unharmed. He shouted his bravery and skill at the crowd and then at the cow. The cow, seeing his gestures as further provocation, pawed to charge again. The youth decided that he had done his bit and it was time for some more beer, and so before the cow had dropped its head he had scaled the stockade.

The cow looked around for alternative targets. But the other youths were not quite as adventurous, and for the next few minutes the cow just charged backwards and forwards, never getting within ten feet of the fleeing matadors.

The organizers decided it was time for the professional

bullfighter to come on. His traditional costume was a tacky affair of gold and red in mock satin. He was smothered in advertising for the local beer, Ducal. Even his red cloak had Ducal emblazoned across it in gold letters.

The cloak was partially wrapped round the hilt of a long sword. Holding the ornate handle, he swirled the sword around his head, the cloak billowing theatrically. The crowd cheered and clapped as he strutted at the half-exhausted cow. The cow pawed the dust, dropped her head and charged. Our matador took a few faltering steps and just managed to hop out of the cow's path. As an afterthought, he swirled the cloak in the direction of the passing bovine. Delighted with the applause at his success, he faced the cow with increased confidence. With a surprising show of determination the cow charged another half a dozen times. The matador, still learning on the job, sidestepped and parried with increasing agility.

The cow, now thoroughly exhausted and demoralized, gave up and stood snorting heavily, with flecks of blood coming out of its nostrils. Even a few half-bricks thrown from the crowd didn't rouse it into action. The brave beast had been debased for the transitory pleasure of a crowd.

Our matador approached to within ten feet and knelt, paying homage to his combatant, this gesture proving his domination over the cow. The crowd roared at his victory and he saluted them pompously, raising aloft his cloak-shrouded sword.

At this moment of ultimate triumph, his cloak slipped out of his over-enthusiastic grasp. It slid from the sword revealing the jewel-encrusted pommel to be connected to a wooden blade. Carried away in his victorious euphoria, he brandished his child's toy aloft until the crowd's derision sunk through his battle fatigue. He stared at the cloak lying crumpled in the dirt. Standing legs spread and motionless he couldn't believe the cruelty of his fate. He looked up at his raised sword to confirm his worst nightmare; his fraud exposed to all. Dignity lost for ever, he scooped up his cloak and ran from the stockade, the crowd howling with laughter.

The lorry arrived again and deposited another trussed cow. There were loud murmurs of disappointment. The locals standing beside me told me that this year's mayor was a cheapskate. They recounted to me that the mayor of two years ago had really splashed out, buying two ferocious bulls. A couple of the local youths had been caught out by the quality of these imported bulls and had been trampled to death. The crowd standing around me nodded their testimony to the truth of this story, and smiled at the memory of one hell of a carnival.

The fresh cow untied, the whole procedure started again. The drunk returned to have another go, and this time, in an increased state of intoxication, he was not so fortunate. The third time the cow knocked him to the ground there was a teeth-grating snap as his arm took the full impact of half a ton of future beef burgers. The other youths were not as prepared to risk death after this demonstration of fast-food, brute destruction. The disgraced matador was forced to take on a slightly fresher cow, but there was no more excitement so I wandered off to sit on the grass with Anita.

That evening the whole plaza was filled with games and singing. A band set up their instruments on the central stand. Another party exclusive to *cumparsa* members was held in the hall. The young women dressed up in regional costumes and danced solo around the floor to the accompaniment of the appropriate tunes. The finale of the show was the carnival queen's dance. She was led around the dance floor by representatives of each *cumparsa*, the custom being that anyone could have an excuse me. I toyed with the idea of leading her in a little break-dancing but decided the locals might disapprove. This party ended fairly early and we all went out to join the throngs in the plaza.

The band was playing and anyone who wanted to sing

could go up and give it a bash. One set of proud parents pushed up their young daughter. There was an unfortunate choice of song as the picture of a six-year-old trying to express the heartbreak of unrequited love brought everyone to tears of laughter.

The Sunday was the climax of the carnival for another year. Many of the transient party goers had departed for Santa Cruz, leaving the true locals to wind up the carnival. Each *cumparsa* meets for its own private party

Huacha met in the butcher's back yard. Crates of beer were stacked against the wall and we tucked in. There was also a four-man band who played the monotonous Bolivian notes on guitar and drums. People ran around with bowls and buckets of water and within minutes everyone was soaked. We danced hand in hand in a ring, first in one direction and then the other, constantly bombarded with water bombs. After a couple of hours of beer, water and Bolivian ring-a-ring-a-roses, we linked hands in groups of threes and fours and danced out into the street. All the *cumparsas* had miraculously co-ordinated their entry into the streets.

We converged on to the plaza with *Huacha,* the most energetic, leading the multicoloured procession, and other *cumparsas* joining in at the rear. Two or three hundred people of all ages wearing brightly coloured *cumparsa* shirts danced in line, each competing for volume in their chants. Predictably, *Bomba Huacha* echoed above the rest. All the *cumparsas'* individual bands joined the procession and played in discordant unison.

The dance was very easy to grasp. My partners of Anita, Charo and another girl linked hands and ran forward. Swinging our arms as if we were running into a wild wind, we would stop and be forced back. We would stumble back a few steps before rallying to surge forward again. The entire line surged and fell back in forced unison for, if you didn't respond to the general movement, you would be squashed. With about eight *cumparsas* of approximately thirty members of all ages, we made a joyful procession.

We circled together and tighter until we converged on the centre of the plaza. The Greens led the whole village and *Huacha* climbed the steps of the fulcrum of the plaza, the bandstand. We joined hands making a circle and danced on the bandstand round first to the right and then to the left. The other *cumparsas* linked hands in circles around us.

All the *cumparsas* formed concentric circles and danced in the opposite direction to the circles closest to them. The bands played to a crescendo, the drummers thumping out the rhythm of our steps and then, at the moment of maximum volume everyone charged into the centre, constricting the circles to a large knot of brightly dressed people. Everyone cheered and kissed.

It was an incredible finale to the carnival and I drifted away with my hand resting lightly on Anita's bottom, wondering where else in the world a near stranger to local customs, problems and trials could find such willingness to share their infrequent pleasures. That day, in that small town, there were no strangers, they shared their joy with such generosity. We celebrated life, life with starvation instead of European food mountains; poverty instead of microwaves and videos. Yet, they still found enough to celebrate about. It did not just stir emotions, it kicked them up the backside. It was magic!

CHAPTER 21

*

Cocaine

February was a nice month. I had no work to do in the park. Robin and Guy were involved in writing reports so I spent my time at my own leisure.

I'd wake late and go and sit on the veranda with the air rifle and shoot down a couple of grapefruit for breakfast. I could quite easily have picked them from the tree, but somehow a half hour hunting the breakfast increased my enjoyment. After an omelette for lunch I'd stroll up to the plaza. I'd either spend the afternoon with Dennis at the priest's house or with the local youths. We would play volleyball in the school yard.

I would walk back to the Whitehouse and change for the evening and then amble back to the plaza. One of the locals had decided to continue her foodstall after the carnival and Delsie, the hotel owner and main socialite of the village, also started to serve meals. I had a choice of meal for about sixty pence.

Without television the local youth would sit around the plaza in the warm night playing their guitars and singing. I now knew them all well. I would spend the evening trying to lure Anita into the shadows. Her mother would shout across the plaza and tell her to come home. It was an uncomplicated, if somewhat frustrating, lifestyle.

I decided to entice Anita down to Santa Cruz. Unprocessed chocolate pods were clearly not enough. The vibrance of the big city lights might nurture the romance. It was on one of these outings that the danger of infidelity was forcefully demonstrated.

Waking in my Santa Cruz hotel from my afternoon siesta there were still two hours until Anita arrived. I decided to go for a drink and so I headed for a bar on the central plaza. I sat at one of their roadside tables sipping beer and watched the early evening hustle and bustle. The plaza was full of people going out, going home or just standing chatting. I noticed an exquisite woman sitting alone at the neighbouring table. I smiled at her and looked away. After what I considered a cool length of time I looked back. She smiled and so I said hello. She looked a ripe eighteen-year-old. She forwardly asked if she could join me. As she stood up to walk over I realized she had every right to be forward. Her figure would not only have turned a monk's head, it would have given him whiplash. To excuse her forwardness she explained that she was waiting for a lift home and that she was always hassled if she waited alone. I nodded sympathetically, although my ego considered this a rather feeble line. I ordered her a drink and we chatted happily away, becoming familiar surprisingly quickly.

She told me about her family and that she lived quite close. Maybe I could call for her one day? The invitation was unusual. Normally I would need a character reference from the Pope to take a girl out. I must have stumbled across a liberated South American. Through her tight T-shirt I could clearly see she wasn't wearing a bra. That was a pity, as I would gladly have helped her set fire to it. I limbered up mentally.

She was fiddling with two black and white photographs and I discovered that they were photos of herself as a young girl which she'd been showing to her grandmother. I asked to see them. She laughed embarrassed, as if she didn't want to show them. As I stretched over to take them, my hand rested significantly on hers. She made no attempt to move it, so I left it there and gazed into her eyes. Her pupils were wildly dilated. She was either overloaded with passion or drugged out of her head. Even my imaginative ego couldn't believe I had such a spontaneous physical effect. She must be floating on a dust cloud.

Being within a mile of drugs was too close for me. For a gringo, it was suicidal. She asked if I wanted one of the photos. I said no, explaining that if my girl-friend found me with a photo of another girl I'd be in trouble. She put them away in her handbag.

While I was thinking of a polite way to escape, she crossed her long legs, her short skirt riding up seductively. She flicked her hair with a languid stroke of her hand, her bumps jutting so far out that I imagined they might go off. *This girl knows all the tricks,* I thought.

This behaviour, however, put me even more on guard. She was too good; she must be a professional. I had hoped the mention of girlfriend would move her on, but she was intent on staying. I noticed she was twirling a little scent bag around her finger, and I asked her what it was.

'*Droga,*' she replied. I told her I didn't want any as it was bad news for a gringo. The situation was deteriorating rapidly. I called for my bill. The tables around us were now crowded and the waitress was rushed off her feet. The girl stuck her finger in the bag and pulled it out with an even centimetre depth of cocaine resting along its length. 'Here, it's just a little drugs.'

Conscious of the crowd, I said, 'Get lost!' as venomously as I could.

I looked about for the waitress. My head turned away from the girl, she shoved the open bag over my nose. I gasped, involuntarily snorting two full nostrils of cocaine. My head was engulfed by a cloud of white dust. I swore at her and went into the bar. I threw a large note at the waitress and walked back out into the street. The girl had disappeared into the crowd. I rushed back to my hotel room and locked myself in. I lay on the bed staring at the door. It seemed to be moving further and further away as if it was at the end of a long corridor. I splashed my face with cold water and lay back on the bed. My eyes were constantly drawn back to the sinking door. I looked at my watch every few minutes, expecting at least half an hour had passed since I last looked.

The phone shocked me into action. It was reception telling me Anita was here. I said she could come up. No longer alone, I was able to relax and the drug actually made contact exquisite. It's not to be recommended, however, as it seriously affects performance. Unfortunately, I didn't know the Spanish for headache.

I met Paolo the next day and explained what had happened. He told me that several girls worked the plaza in league with corrupt police. They preyed on tourists and foreign businessmen who would be lured by the prospect of sex or cocaine. Five minutes after taking the bait the police would arrive at your room. The girl would conveniently disappear and you would be left with a room full of cocaine.

He knew of someone who had been caught out. The person had not gone to prison, however, as a couple of thousand dollars had smoothed formalities. It seemed one hell of a racket, and I had very nearly been conned by it.

I decided to stay as far away from strange women as hormonally possible. This wasn't a difficult choice as Anita now dominated my thoughts.

*

CHAPTER 22

Desperdido

Back in Buena Vista life moved slowly. The social high-light of my week was spending a particularly loud evening with Pablo in his shed. He was celebrating the birth of yet another son. Handing me an opened bottle of beer, he went to fetch the baby so I could admire it.

He kept it in a homemade crib on top of the fridge. He offered me the bundled sheet. I put down my beer and briefly studied this pink, wrinkly thing. Although it looked quite disgusting, I duly congratulated him. His bucolic face flushed crimson and a shy grin spread across his proud, beetroot cheeks. He dropped the baby back in the crib and we opened another crate of beer.

He didn't have a name for it, so we thought long and hard for the next five hours. Suddenly, as I swallowed another bottle, inspiration hit me. 'Oliver! Call it Oliver!'

He stared at me incredulously, then hiccupped and started to giggle. Calling a Bolivian baby 'Oliver' is comparable with calling on English baby 'Rodriguez' or 'Chingo'. In his intoxicated state, the absurdity appealed. He retrieved the pink bundle again, and with it slung under his arm, he swayed round the yard, introducing it, between belches, to his friends, 'Meet my baby, Oliver.'

His wife was furious and snatched it back. She severely reprimanded Pablo for his careless handling of the baby. He sank down on a chair very sullen-faced. However, as soon as she had gone inside, Pablo started chuckling, his rotund girth wobbling in synchrony. The wife reappeared red-faced at the doorway and sent us all home. Everyone staggered off leaving her angry shouts lashing Pablo into bed.

The next morning I slept late. I managed to jump start my brain with the promise of food. I pushed back my eyelids and a blurred shape gradually came into focus. I froze, horrified. Two inches above my nose hung a large, nasty looking scorpion. I managed to manoeuvre out from underneath it. It hung by a single spider's thread from the bookshelf. I prodded it with a pencil. It was dead.

Above my purple sofa on this shelf lived a large spider. I had christened him Barny. I had always intended to relocate Barny and dump him out in the garden. However, I never plucked up the courage to face him.

I spotted my arachnid chum sitting on the shelf. He must have fought the scorpion to the death. Barny had not had it all his own way, however, as he was missing a couple of legs. He had hung the scorpion up in what he presumed was his pantry for later consumption.

Confident the scorpion was dead, I was brave enough to taunt it with my finger. Meanwhile Guy had come in.

'Don't touch it!'

'What?' I demanded, angry at the command.

'We'll put it in a jar for the Santa Cruz museum,' said the never-off-duty biologist.

Much to Barny's annoyance, Guy carefully deposited the scorpion in an alcohol-filled jar.

In an attempt to console Barny, and as a reward for his fearless protection, I granted him a lifetime reprieve. Every morning I would find him guarding me, seated proudly on his bookshelf.

To calm my frayed nerves I went up to Pablo's to see if he had survived the night. I noticed he had a new dog chained up in his yard.

'Pablo, what happened to your other dog?'

'I shot it.'

Stunned, I asked, 'Why?'

'It had rabies.'

'Oh.'

Ask a silly question. This was a well-repeated scenario. What it usually meant was that someone had forgotten to feed the dog. It grew hungry and therefore bad tempered. All bad-tempered dogs are diagnosed rabid and shot.

I took a bottle of beer and sat on my usual plank at the front of the barn. One of the locals joined me, as he noticed I had a full packet of cigarettes. We chatted about his crops.

In the distance a bent figure waivered in the afternoon heat. Out of the haze the silhouette developed definition. A weighted frame trudged towards us, its head bowed and back arched under a roughly hewn plank; a man, his clothes tattered and dirty. He wore no shoes. There was nothing strange about his clothes or his emaciated state, but he exuded pain. His tiny body was perspiring with grief.

Behind him, hand in hand, walked his daughters, two beautiful girls of around three and five years old. Their faces and hair were scrubbed until they shone. The elder wore a pink dress, complete with white lace, and her brown hair was tied up with pink ribbons in two pigtails. Her little sister had an identical yellow dress and yellow ribbons. A great deal of care had been taken to dress them. It seemed particularly odd, as it was still only early afternoon. Despite their beautiful dresses, their poverty was unmistakable. They wore no shoes or socks and their feet had a bronzed sturdiness that suggested they had never known the confinement of either. They followed their solemn father, his mood casting a shroud over their youth.

The family group paced slowly past, never looking up. They walked on into the hut next to Pablo's. I had no idea anyone lived there, as even by Bolivian standards it looked derelict. Much of the palm roof had fallen in and the mud walls were crumpled and decayed.

I turned to my neighbour to ask about this strange procession. He had not spoken since he first saw them on the road. He said, 'He's making a coffin for his baby.'

I asked what she had died of.

He replied, 'Malnutrition.'

I had become used to seeing poverty but sitting there I was horrified. What could it possibly cost to feed a baby? Right next door to where that baby had died, evening after evening, I had spent more on beer than it would cost to feed a baby for over a week. All the times I had come here that baby was dying while I sat yards away laughing and drinking. The pitiful family had watched their child die, while my drunken shouts had invaded their home through the decayed walls.

I knew it was ridiculous to feel responsible, but, challenged by this absolute waste of human life, it was hard to remain aloof. It disturbed the precarious equilibrium of my Western ideals. It was difficult to see the importance of seven per cent pay claims and European free markets. I hoped that I would always think like this, but I knew as soon as I was back in England it would be just another nameless death a long way away.

I left my beer and went to see Dennis. He also had a hard time adjusting to the poverty. What he found particularly frightening was how easy it was to accept it and become almost blasé.

Dennis and I spent a great deal of time philosophizing. He was leaving Bolivia to return to America in a couple of weeks. He had almost come to a decision about which religious order he wanted to join. It was now a toss up between the Jesuits and the Benedictine monks. We had lengthy discussions about both. My opinion was that he should be a Jesuit as I believed a monk's life to be a waste. He said that dedicating your life to prayer was the purest generosity. I considered it selfish as you didn't do anything for anyone else. I told him he was just guaranteeing his own ticket on the heaven train. He answered that there was no way of measuring the benefit to the world of collective prayer.

He always answered my affirmations with calm patience.

All this Catholicism was new to me as I had grown up in Belfast on the Protestant side of the fence. Not being religious, I had hoped to have avoided most of the sectarian prejudices. However, some must have rubbed off. In my conversations, I held Dennis responsible for my vision of the inadequacies of Catholicism, and in particular the Pope's insistence on the evil of contraception, which I believe has contributed greatly to the epidemic spread of AIDS in Africa.

Dennis answered all my allegations eloquently, never losing his temper, as I attacked every aspect of his religion. Considering this was not only his religion but what he was dedicating his life to, his patience was astounding. I was greatly impressed with the strength of his belief. I envied his utter faith. His devotion gave him a purpose. His whole life was plotted, and the path led him to his God. He sacrificed much but he was glad to do it. He also never tried to convert me. However, he prayed for me and reassured me that God would be there if I needed him.

During one of these gargantuan discussions we were sitting in the Whitehouse. I noticed a few ants over by my sofa. That was not unusual except that they looked black and red. I walked over to investigate. True enough they were army ants. I went into the bedroom where a couple of thousand were swarming across the floor. Out in the garden a huge procession was marching with unstoppable determination. For ten minutes Dennis and I tried to deflect them away from the house. Armed with two brooms, we tried to sweep them away. The soldiers with their huge jaws ran up the broom handles to attack our hands. It was useless. We resigned the house to them, and within minutes millions were pouring over everything.

Dennis had driven down in one of the priests' jeeps. I grasped this opportunity to pile it high with the chocolate tree's last pods. Dennis was curious why I was taking orange-coloured pods to my girl-friend.

'The sap surrounding the cocoa seeds is supposed to

have even stronger aphrodisiac qualities than the final product, chocolate,' I replied, with a large wink.

As usual my intentions were lost on Dennis. 'Oh, is that where chocolate comes from?'

'No, Dennis. Willy Wonka makes it with a magic wand.'

'Well, I didn't know.' We loaded the car and set off for the village. After a couple of minutes Dennis turned with a puzzled look, 'Willy Who?'

'Willy Wonka.'

'Who's he?'

'The Managing Director of Cadbury's.'

I joined Dennis for a fresh lemonade at the priest's house. Padre Paul told me it is considered lucky to have your house invaded by army ants as they clean away all the cockroaches. I just hoped they would move on and not take up residence.

Anita was out, so I left the amorous fruit pods piled up on her dinner table. I was gradually weaning her off normal food and on to a more productive diet. When I returned to the Whitehouse the ants had gone. True enough the house was spotless. They had eaten all the cockroaches and house-crickets. Sadly, they had also taken Barny, my bookshelf spider. I never saw him again.

Guy was out so I sat on my sofa and mourned the passing of Barny. Silent and alone, my thoughts meandered round and round until I could think of no other diversion. I had been avoiding the subject for weeks but my apathy had now broken. I needed to make a decision about my future.

For me the work in the park was over. The wet season had stopped all field trips. I had neither the experience nor the qualifications to help with scientific papers. My money was gradually whittling away and, although I never felt time moving in this remote existence, I knew out there, in the real world, it was marching on. For the last six months I had never known what day of the week it was. Occasionally, if the wind was blowing in the right direction, I might hear the faint chiming of the church bells

calling all for Sunday Mass, but apart from that I was cut
off from real time. It had been heaven to live my life at
my own pace, but it was also disorientating. I imagined
my family back in England growing grey and wrinkly.

I knew I had sucked this experience dry and I was sitting
in yet another rut. This rut was preferable to the building
society, but it was starting to feel equally confining. I
realized the only things keeping me here were the fear of
an unknown destination and Anita.

My destination could be tackled easily. Via a heavily
distorted phone call I learned my father wanted to meet
me in Peru in a couple of weeks. He wanted to combine
seeing me and vising Machu Picchu (The Lost City of the
Incas). If I met him I could have a rest from Bolivia and
make up my mind whether or not to return. I certainly
wasn't ready to return to England. The alternative I was
considering was to visit my uncle in New Zealand.

Anita, on the other hand, was a big problem. I would
never be able to find paid employment in Bolivia, therefore
inside Bolivia there could never be a future for us. Outside
Bolivia I could never support her. Thinking about her and
what my uncertain future held, I realized I would have to
make a clean break. I would tell her now. I sat on the sofa
for another two hours.

She met me at her doorway, another short skirt, still as
desirable. I led her by the hand to find a cool place away
from the afternoon heat. Buena Vista was in a considerate
siesta. The streets were lifeless, the inhabitants in sensible
slumber. Even the recumbent dogs did no more than blink
as we strolled silently past, my mind searching for the
words.

We sat on the luxuriant grass bank under the church.
Holding my hand she sensed something was wrong. She
held back her natural exuberance and waited for me to
speak. I had prepared four or five alternative speeches.
My mind did a blank; my tongue felt thick. I chickened
out.

'Anita, I'm going to Peru, to meet my father.'

'When are you going?'

'In just over a week.'

'When will you come back?' she asked. Her voice quivered with timorous uncertainty.

'I don't know.' I owed her better than this. I took the plunge.

'I don't think I'm coming back.'

I tried to explain about the work in the park and that there was nothing left for me to do. I could never get a job to earn money. She asked me to stay. I said I couldn't. She begged me to ask Robin if he could get me a job. I knew the political position of the park. Robin had a hard time justifying voluntary workers; paid employment would be impossible. She cried. I held her, hugged her until she wept herself dry.

Over the next week the scene was repeated many times. She tried anger, stamping her foot and swinging at me with tiny clenched fists. But it always ended with her crying in my unworthy arms. It was a long week.

To meet my father I would have to leave just before her eighteenth birthday. As a passing gesture I gave her the bracelet I had bought for my sister in São Paulo. She again pleaded with me to stay, but now her tempers were more controlled. A slightly trembling lip softened her decisive features. She looked up with a brave yet slightly moist stare. 'I want to cook you a meal before you go.'

On the appointed day I made myself as smart as my old Bic razor and my wheelbarrow-washed clothes would allow. I strolled up to her house, my spit-polished shoes collecting sand with every step. Anita greeted me at her doorway with a customary kiss on the cheek. She wore the cocktail dress I had given her and she held out her wrist for me to admire my sister's bracelet.

'My mother's only just gone out so I didn't have time to buy anything special to eat.' Her mother still frowned on our relationship. I assured her anything would be

lovely. She sat me at table and poured me a glass of beer.
The table was only set for one.

'Aren't you eating?'

She shook her head and turned away.

'No, this is just for you.'

She left me in the bare room and went through to the
house's only other room – the kitchen and double bedroom
where she slept with her mother and sister. I smoked a
sedating cigarette while cooking noises and smells wafted
into the room.

A couple of minutes later she returned, a plate in her
hand. She placed it in front of me, never taking her eyes
from mine, searching for my impressions. I smiled and
looked down. Such had been the quality of the Bolivian
cuisine that even eggs and chips was a feast.

'This is great,' and I meant it.

Throughout the meal she stood over me, watching me
gorge. When I had finished she kissed me. 'I love you.'

'Yes, I thought you did,' I replied, a little numb.

'Who told you?' she answered smiling. I smiled and we
laughed together. I grasped this moment to give her a
present. I gave her my mother's gold-framed amethyst
from the jeweller's in Rio. I still had the receipt so I could
always tell my mother it had been stolen. Anita studied it
demurely and thanked me. She said, however, she still
preferred the bracelet. I thought it might be uncool to tell
her that the bracelet was worthless and the jewel cost over
a month's Bolivian wages.

At that moment she broke, a storm of tears flooding
from some hidden reservoir. I wiped the puddles from her
eyes.

'I don't want you to go.'

'I know.'

'Stay with me, you can get a job.'

'I can't.'

'Please don't go.'

'Anita, I have to go. I have no future.'

She lifted her chin and through tight lips she whispered, 'I know.' At last she had accepted it.

Over the next few days I started a round of goodbyes. Delsie, the one-bedroom hotel owner, found out that Dennis and I were leaving and she decided to throw us a *Desperdido,* a Bolivian leaving party. She invited Padre Paul and Padre Tom, Dennis and me for the meal. Her two sons also joined us for the food. Anita looked beautiful with my mother's amethyst around her delicate neck. After the religious people left we all got rather drunk. It was the first tearless night in a week.

Guy and Robin thanked me for my help and I thanked them for the opportunity. I said I wasn't sure when or if I would be back. Guy and I were poles apart in character. He was a bit of an intellectual, a conservationist to his very core. I was a ducking and diving city kid gone green. We had found common ground in our love for nature. The rigours of our shared hardships in the jungle had developed our friendship. I respected his knowledge and dedication. I gave him my canvas trousers.

Robin was grateful for my help and wished me well. He had been in Bolivia a long time and had seen many people come and go. I knew he would carry on fighting against all the odds to preserve what he considered his garden.

I packed my bags, said 'Kuchy-koo' to Oliver the Second, paid my bar bill and waved *'Adiós'* to Buena Vista.

*

CHAPTER 23

Interpol

Anita wanted to see me off down in Santa Cruz but was scared of letting her mother know, so we caught the micro in different places. We booked straight into a hotel and then went to the cinema. On returning to the hotel, Anita rang her cousin's house to concoct an alibi for her mother. Her mother answered the phone. She had smelled foul play and had followed us down to Santa Cruz. Anita told her mother that she was just with friends and would come straight over. She would try to get back to me by nine-thirty. By ten she had still not reappeared. My double bed seemed awfully big.

But then she arrived. She had obviously been crying for some time. She also had bruises on her arms where her mother had hit her. Her mother had forbidden her to go out. She had run away. I said she must go back and face the music. No, there was to be no arguing, first thing the next morning she must go back. I comforted her as best I could.

I lay awake the next morning as the light peeped through the window. I knew I had to leave Bolivia and I wouldn't be coming back. I could never come back. Take her with me? Impossible. I didn't even know where I was going. Her world was Buena Vista and Santa Cruz. She knew nothing else. She had never seen the sea, felt the touch of snow or drunk a pint of Guinness.

It would be fantastic to show her London, Paris, Bognor Regis. We could fly in planes, dive on the Great Barrier Reef, eat lobster on the Greek Islands. Dream on. She didn't even have a passport. She would be lost in the outside world. Here she was cherished by family and friends.

Her head was resting on my chest, her breathing erratic. She was pretending to be asleep. I gave her a hug. She immediately started crying, her tears trickling down my arm.

Oh God, I have to stop this! I got up and told her to get dressed.

'Anita, you have to go home.'

She rubbed red eyes.

'I'm leaving Bolivia.'

'I'm not coming back.'

She was crying freely now, sobbing into my chest. I pushed her away.

'Go.'

She stood trembling, biting back the tears. I opened the door, 'Go, please.'

Through the sobs she forced out a request,

'Look after yourself. If not for you, do it for me.' Then she turned away and ran, crying, out of my life.

'I will always remember you,' stuck in my throat.

I sat back on the bed and brushed a tear from my chin. It must be one of hers. After half a packet of cigarettes I lay back to get some sleep. No chance. I started talking to myself, 'There you go, thinking with your trousers got you into this.' I smoked another cigarette, 'I should never have started with her.' I knew I didn't believe that.

The phone rang. It was reception. Two men from Interpol were here to see me. 'That's all I bloody need!'

I picked up my passport and locked my door. Down in reception, I recognized the casual clothes and gold jewellery. They led me to a small alcove off the foyer. I sat down. One sat opposite me and the other sat next to me. They sat in silence as they studied my passport. They checked the stamps.

They worked out that I had been on the train to Brazil,

considered a major cocaine smuggling route. They commented to each other about my route through South America. They suggested it was odd that I was back and staying in the hotel most used by the smugglers. I realized this conversation was for my benefit. They were softening me up. Holding my passport accusingly they turned to confront me.

'Where's your cocaine?'

'How much did you take on the train to Brazil?'

'Who were you with last night?'

'Did you pay her?'

'Who gave you the cocaine?'

'Tell us the truth. It will be easier in the long run.'

They fired the questions at me. This was no good cop bad cop routine. They were both bad cops. My interrogators took turns in questioning me. I was quickly becoming disorientated. They sat inches from me, their eyes staring, their mouths accusing.

'Why do you take cocaine?'

'What do you smuggle for?'

'How much money do you make?'

'Have you been convicted?'

They disregarded my stumbling Spanish answers.

'Is that why you are in Bolivia?'

'What do you really do in Bolivia?'

I tried to tell them about the park. They wouldn't listen. They moved closer until they were touching me. With increased venom they started again. The spittle from their odious mouths flicked into my eyes.

'Where is your cocaine?'

'Is it in your room?'

'We know you've got cocaine!'

'Don't lie to us!'

'Where is your cocaine?'

'Where have you hidden it?'

'We will find it!'

'Where did you get your cocaine?'

Then came the crunch.

'How much money do you have?'

'I have nothing!'

They smiled and started again. 'Where is your cocaine?'

They had been questioning me for half an hour. I knew I would soon break.

'How much cocaine have you got?'

'What is it worth?'

I breathed in deeply and looked the boss straight in the eye. 'I don't touch cocaine. I don't sell cocaine. I don't have cocaine! I have nothing! nothing! nothing!'

They looked at each other and conferred. The one sitting opposite whispered, 'I say we take him off to test his blood. He's on cocaine.'

The boss turned and studied me carefully. 'We will be back at six o'clock tonight. Think it over. By then we want answers!'

They left me shellshocked. The fear and adrenalin started to make me shake. I went up and searched my room from top to bottom. Nothing had been planted. I locked the door and went looking for the British Consulate.

I felt so alone and vulnerable. Fear brought out instincts – fight or flight. I would fight.

Out on the street the hairs on the back of my neck tingled. Although I never spotted anyone, I was sure I was being followed. I eventually found the consulate. The consul was very busy. I told the receptionist I wouldn't move until I'd seen him. After an hour I was admitted.

He was an American businessman who earned a few extra dollars by running a part-time consulate. I explained what had happened to me and he sceptically took down my name and contacts. He clearly didn't want to be involved in any drug problems. I could understand his misgivings as most of the foreigners are involved with the cocaine. Fortunately for me he remembered meeting my father on his visit. He said, however, that he was leaving town that afternoon and couldn't be with me when they returned. He would give me some advice instead.

He said firstly that on no account should I see them in my room. They were prone to drop sachets of cocaine and then, while searching, they would rediscover them and say they belonged to me. If they insisted on searching my room, I was to ask the receptionist to accompany me to decrease the likelihood of such an accident. I should also make a note of their names. There were many con men posing as police officers in order to get bribes. Even if they were real Interpol, this was certainly no guarantee of their honesty.

I had now virtually convinced him of my innocence and he agreed to write me a character note. On the back of his introduction card he wrote that my father and I were known to the British Consulate and that my father had worked for the British Mission. His wife who worked as his secretary said that on no account should I let them take me anywhere. Once I agreed to go I was totally in their power and would just disappear. She also kindly gave me her home number should there be any further problems and told me to ring after Interpol had left to make sure I was all right. I thanked them and caught a taxi to the museum.

Paolo kindly agreed to come over to my hotel at half-past five to lend moral support and possible translation. My Spanish had been stretched to the absolute limit in the previous interrogation. It seemed an unnecessarily stressful way to learn a language. I went back to my hotel and searched it from top to bottom. I was working myself up for the confrontation. I would be ready for the bastards!

Just after four my telephone rang. There was a friend at reception for me, could he come up? Paranoia was closing in, I sensed a trap.

Fortunately it was only Chingo, a friend from Buena Vista. He said that Anita was missing and that no one had seen her since last night. Had I seen her?

'I haven't seen her since I left Buena Vista,' I lied.

'Her mother thinks she is with you, and if she doesn't come back soon her mother is going to call the police.'

Fortunately Anita's mother didn't know where I was or she would already have been round. The police could imprison me for sleeping with a girl under twenty-one. Normally no notice is taken of this law. However, if a gringo is involved, a bribe may be possible.

With Interpol trying to frame me for cocaine possession and smuggling, I considered this last bit of news a trifle unfair. I had visions of a shotgun wedding with the shotgun being replaced with a threatened prison sentence. I'd had enough of Bolivia. It was time to leave. The sooner I got out, the sooner Anita could get on with the rest of her life. I went to the travel agent and booked a flight to Peru for the next morning.

Interpol never turned up, which was probably a good thing as in my cornered state of mind I probably would have tried to kill them. I can only assume they followed me to the consulate and decided I was innocent or unprepared to pay.

Paolo took me for a farewell meal. I met one of Anita's friends. There was still no sign of her and the police had been informed. I spent a worried and nervous night alone in my hotel.

I left Bolivia the next morning without saying goodbye to Anita. I had no phone number to ring, no address to send a note. She'd been missing for twenty-four hours. I didn't know where she was or even whether she was alive or dead.

CHAPTER 24

*

Peru

The stresses of South American travel distracted me. I had to be totally absorbed in watching my bags, my money, looking for dangers and working out what to do. I shut out all thoughts of what I'd left behind and concentrated on what was ahead. Lima was my destination and that's all I needed to know.

At the information desk in Lima airport I asked the average price of a taxi to the centre. Typically they had their own taxi, and at ten dollars it seemed reasonable. They called over the driver and I loaded him with my bags.

His car was an absolute relic. To my amazement it chugged into life and we bunny-hopped along, backfiring contentedly. Only a few miles out of the airport smoke started to spew from the dashboard. My driver waved it away unperturbed and stuck his head out of the window so that he could see where he was going. The smoke grew thicker and billowed through the car. I was coughing so violently I couldn't speak. I managed to croak, 'Stop!'

He pulled over and I piled out, wondering whether to dive for cover. He saw I was a little unsure and so he tried to comfort me.

'Don't worry, it's only the wiring.'

Well of course my mind was immediately put at ease. My driver fought the flames to a flicker and bundled me back in, assuring me the firework display was over.

We drove on towards the city. At the sides of the wide roads were trees sculptured from car exhausts. The driver explained that they belonged to the unofficial mechanics who arranged the exhausts to attract custom. The mechanics couldn't afford premises or taxes, so they worked at the side of the road.

As we sat in a queue waiting for the traffic lights to change, young boys darted between the line of cars, wiping windscreens and demanding money. The lights changed before they arrived at our soot-encrusted dragster. The engines revved and burned away, disregarding the waifs as they desperately ran for the safety of the pavements. Dozens of boys are churned up by indifferent wheels each year.

My sinuses, cleared of molten wire fumes, breathed in the city. Lima stank. The pungent reek of urine filled my lungs. It hasn't rained in Lima since 1972 and the old sandstone buildings and streets have absorbed the smell. The aggressive heat from the bleaching sun intensified the stench.

I imagined my father would appreciate this taxi driver and his car as a caricature representative of South America. I told him to meet my father's flight and bring him to the hotel. I spent the rest of the day making my father's drinks bill look respectable.

He arrived the next afternoon to find me still sitting in the hotel bar. It struck me how white he was; other than that he seemed unchanged. However, he was horrified by me. Our reunion was tempered by his concern for my appearance. I had wasted away from thirteen stones to ten. I assured him my diminutive stature was nothing serious.

After much persuasion he agreed to spend the afternoon sightseeing. At a museum some young girls flirted round us. My complete lack of interest was the final straw. My father believed I must have a terminal illness – all this weight-loss and not being interested in girls. He curtailed our exploration and over the next three days he dragged me to several clinics for tests. After x-rays and all sorts of intimate investigations, we discussed the results with the hotel doctor. He said I was extremely malnourished and just needed careful feeding. I was greatly relieved that I didn't have any lasting disease, as the memory of the yellow-fever needle was still jutting infectiously in my arm.

Satisfied that I would recover, we set about having a good time. On a hotel tour of the city, we were shown the presidential palace and the city convent. In the convent the guide led us through small corridors and down decaying stairways until we were in the dark bowels of the ancient building. As we were led through these catacombs, my father and I brought up the rear. Peering through a small hole in the passage wall I noticed a hidden cellar, piled high with bones. Among them were human ribcages and skulls. We heard the guide explain that we were now entering the city's old cemetery. Up to a hundred years ago the people of the city had brought their dead to the convent for entombment. The ground was so hard that conventional burial was impossible. Instead they had just been thrown down into these cellars. It had been estimated that there were over eighty thousand bodies in these vaults stretching back four hundred years.

He led on. The narrow path was now raised and on each side there were open pits full of bones. The remarkable thing was that they were not complete bodies. Each pit contained different parts of the skeletons. One pit for femurs, one for arms, one for skulls and some of these stone vats had crumbled strewing the bones on to the path. With a true sense of tourist participation we were expected to dodge the ribcages. There must have been some seriously disturbed nuns to have dismembered and organized the bodies.

We followed the guide into a large chamber. It was explained that this is where the important people were stored. In the bottom of a large, well-like, structure the bones were organized in a circular pattern, the skulls and femurs making concentric circles. In the faint orange light it was all rather ghoulish. The skulls' empty sockets stared, while their toothless jaws grinned at their admirers.

My father was determined to photograph this mock Hades but had unfortunately forgotten his flash. He set his exposure for half a minute and stood holding his camera in stern concentration. Meanwhile the guide led the group back along the corridors. I looked nervously after them.

'Hurry up with the photo!' They had now disappeared back into the maze of tunnels. He stood there, impassive. I was caught in the dilemma of trying to catch up with the tour or stay with my father. Bravely I chose my father. After all, I needed him to pay the hotel bill. By the time he had finished, even the echo of their footsteps was out of earshot. I prayed they didn't turn off the lights. The menacing darkness threatened to envelop us like the jaws of a hungry Minotaur. At last we heard a distant pitfall of feet. It had come just in time before the passage forked. We chased after the sound and tagged on to the end of the tour just as the guide was leading us back above ground.

He turned and smiled at his group. 'Everyone here? Good. I wouldn't want to lose you. There are enough lost souls down there already!'

We all guffawed politely at this standard tour-guide joke, my father and I slightly more enthusiastically than the rest.

That afternoon at a travel agent we booked a tour to Cuzco and Machu Picchu, the Lost City of the Incas. I had decided that I wanted to go on to New Zealand to stay with my uncle. So for my imminent twenty-first birthday, my father bought me a plane ticket to Santiago, Chile. From there I could catch a plane to New Zealand.

Our hotel was right next to St Martín central plaza. During our last afternoon I stood in the square watching a street performer, although I knew this made me a target for pickpockets. In an attempt to limit the danger, I kept my hands firmly in my pockets. In a brief moment of relaxation, I felt a huge wrench on my wrist. I looked down but nothing was touching me. I searched the crowd but no one was moving, and there was no one standing close. It was the fastest attempt at robbery I could imagine. Someone had tried to rip off my watch. The plastic strap had torn but not snapped like a leather or metal one would have done. I was shocked and amazed by the speed of my would-be mugger. I had been on guard, despite it only being early afternoon, and I had still seen no one. My wrist was badly bruised, proving the force of the attempt.

We caught the plane to Cuzco. I was glad to leave the stench and aggression of Lima.

CHAPTER 25

*

Lost City

Cuzco is a mountain city not far from the ruined Inca Machu Picchu. The encyclopedia says Machu Picchu means 'Lost City of the Incas'. However, I didn't believe that the Incas would call a city they had just build 'Lost City of the Incas'. I guessed this had been invented for the tourists, and the more likely translation would be 'Very Hard to Find City of the Incas'.

On the approach to Cuzco the tiny plane navigated between two mountains. It banked sharply, landing with a comfortable ten feet of runway to spare. We were picked up by a courier and taken to our hotel. The air was cold but fresh. Cuzco was the old Inca capital, dominated by a central plaza. One side of this square uses the foundations of the destroyed Inca royal palace.

While exploring the narrow cobbled streets, I saw a man losing his watch. The mugger used a tool that looked like a pair of long scissors with the points bent up. The robber hooked the points under the watch strap and whipped it off. The whole incident had taken less than a couple of seconds and the robber was away before either I or the man could react.

Very early the next morning we were taken to the train station where we caught a tourist train to Machu Picchu. There are two trains that run along this track. The first is the tourist train solely for tourists, which costs about sixty dollars for the return trip. The second is the local train. This costs about two dollars for the return trip. The sixty dollars is money well spent.

The local train is perhaps the most infamous journey in South America. I know of three separate deaths of foreigners in the last couple of years on this train. I have also met one bloke who survived an attack. He was pushed out between the carriages by three locals. They forced him down between the carriages. To survive he let go of his money belt and held on to the guard rail. His body was only inches from being churned by the wheels. His screams brought the train's one guard and the men disappeared. He didn't understand why the men didn't just threaten him with a knife. They seemed intent on killing him. On other occasions I have heard the murderers have succeeded in pushing their victim under the wheels. They have then run back to rob the mutilated body.

Young travellers are attracted by the cheap fares of the local train. They carry with them their cameras, rucksacks and belts of travelling money. They are seen as potential gold mines to the horrendously poor locals. The temptation has proved too great for many, and even those on the train who would not rob, turn a blind eye as the foreigners are bundled from the carriages. No one ever sees anything, yet this is an almost weekly occurrence.

Powering along in the plush security of our locked carriages we passed the local train. It had pulled off into a siding to allow our faster vehicle to pass. A rich American stuck his head out of the window and waved at the locals. As we drew alongside the packed carriages of standing Peruvians, a youth leaned from the window. He reached across the gap and snatched at the American's wrist. He missed grabbing the watch and just knocked the man's waving hand. The American looked back confused, wondering what had hit him. He didn't realize he had just survived an attempted mugging. We were whisked away along the tracks, most of the tourists oblivious to the proximity of brutal poverty.

Pulling into Machu Picchu station, we were immediately loaded on minibuses. These drove us from the valley up the winding ascent. The road was so steep that even the sixteen hairpin bends had to be cut into the mountainside.

I suffer a nose bleed on the second rung of a step ladder, so I put on my sunglasses and closed my eyes. My father kept commenting on the sheer drops and saying, 'Isn't it incredible?'

Behind the flimsy protection of my firmly clamped eyelids I didn't need this continual commentary. I nodded, pretending enthusiasm, 'Yes, it's beautiful.'

We climbed down from the bus and walked the last stretch to the roofless city. I'm not a great one for ruins, especially when they're balanced on crags, but I was moved by the powerful history that had nestled, hidden for centuries, among the timeless mountains. I fought my fear of heights and we explored the all-conquering stonework of the Incas.

The ruined city perches like an inebriated eagle on top of the crumbling mountain. I was left wondering how and why it had ever got there. I can only presume the Inca builders had held the designs upside down and built it on top of the mountain instead of down in the valley. They had succeeded in making it totally self-sufficient: the vegetables were grown on narrow terraces cut into the mountain and the water collected from nearby springs. In the couple of hundred stone buildings had lived a population of around one thousand.

I imagined it would have been a dreadful place in which to grow up. If you were a little careless with your football, you wouldn't sneak round to next door's garden to collect it. Instead you would have to shin down two thousand feet of vertical mountain to search the valley floor.

The guide finally put to rest all doubts about the name Machu Picchu. He told us it means 'Old Peak'. As we stood awestruck by Old Peak, a mist started to envelop the neighbouring mountain, Huayna Picchu (New Peak). Within ten minutes the mist had spread, obscuring all the mountains. Surrounded by vapour in this ancient city and cut off from the world, we felt we were floating in the clouds.

With regret we re-boarded our bus and set off for the trip down. I hoped the brakes worked. As we came round the second hairpin a boy, no more than ten years old, jumped out on to the road. He cheered and waved as we passed. When we came back round the third hairpin he was standing waiting on the road. He waved and cheered again. We watched as he stood waving us into the distance. He then threw himself over the road edge. He reappeared after the next hairpin. I looked up the bank from where he'd emerged and there was a worn slide in the mud and undergrowth. He met us after all but two of the hairpins. I noticed on a couple of his shortcuts that he'd had to clamber down a rope, as it was almost a sheer cliff edge.

Our bus pulled into the station. The boy appeared at the bottom of the mountain and ran a couple of hundred metres across the valley floor to reach the bus just as we were getting off. He stood by the door and held out his hand. He had dropped almost vertically about two thousand feet to the bottom of the mountain. After this show of Olympic athleticism and bravery nearly everyone on the bus forked out. Grinning and barely out of breath, he stuffed the wad of notes into his trousers and waved us goodbye. He set off back towards the mountain. He still had a few hours left to work. If he climbed quickly, he would be at the top ready for another descent in a couple of hours.

Our tour left the train halfway back to Cuzco and boarded a coach. It drove us on an alternative route through the mountains. On the road ahead we came upon a rock fall. The driver didn't slow down but instead he threw the coach into an almost suicidal swerve up the bank. We cleared the boulders with inches to spare. Our guide announced over the tannoy, 'Sorry about that, ladies and gentlemen, but it's best not to stop.'

He offered no further explanation. A Dutchman who

had lived and worked in Peru for the last few years explained. The local guerrillas, who call themselves the *Sendero Luminoso* (Shining Path), stage rock falls to stop tourist buses. Once stopped, they rob and even shoot tourists. The terrorists could have been hiding in the bushes at the side of the road. We were pleased to arrive back in Cuzco free from bullet holes.

We spent the last couple of days sightseeing around Cuzco and picking up some mementoes for the family in the multitude of local craft shops. The street vendors constantly hounded us to buy their beads and carvings. I spotted one little boy with toy llamas for sale. He offered them to a shop owner at the equivalent price of fifty cents each. She was not interested. He walked out into the street and offered one to a tourist for ten dollars. She bought it.

The enterprising youth offered them to us speaking in German. In Spanish I told him we were not interested. He was twelve years old, but he knew how to sell toy llamas in seven different languages.

My father wanted a rug for his front room. The best were made from the fleeces of baby alpacas. The alpacas are a close relative of the llama. We found the one he wanted and I set about to bargain for it. I whispered to my father, 'How much are you prepared to pay?'

'Sixty dollars.'

He slipped me the money.

The shop woman studied us as we looked at her rugs. 'You like rug, señor?'

I replied in Spanish, 'Well it's all right, but it's not quite the right colour. Have you got any others?'

Surprised at my Spanish and my South American accent, she replied, 'I have only got what's there, sir.'

I conferred in English with my father, knowing full well she would understand. 'That's it, I'm afraid. Shall we go somewhere else?'

Before he could respond she interrupted. 'It is a very nice rug, sir. It is baby alpaca.'

I laughed, 'Every one says their rugs are baby alpaca.'

'Sir, for you I give a special price.'

'How much?'

She shook her head and sighed, 'One hundred and twenty dollars.'

To my father, 'They're bound to have more next door.'

'One hundred and ten dollars, señor.'

I snorted, 'Señora, it's a nice rug, but that is far too much.'

'You give me a price, señor.'

I fingered the rug thoughtfully. 'I might pay forty dollars for it.'

'Señor, I am running a business.'

'Fair enough, forty-five dollars.'

'It is worth a hundred dollars, señor.'

'Señora, all the shops sell the same rugs. I can probably get one next door for fifty dollars.'

'Not for fifty dollars.'

To my father, 'Shall we go?'

'Ninety dollars, señor.'

'Señora, you are wasting my time. I'll give you fifty-five dollars.'

'I have a big family, señor, with many mouths to feed. I could not sell it for less than eighty dollars.'

'We all have families, señora. It isn't the right colour, anyway.'

'You drive a hard bargain, señor. It is yours for seventy dollars, even though I will make no profit.'

'Sixty.'

'No, señor. I would lose money. Would you want me to go out of business?' She looked on the verge of weeping.

'Of course not, señora.' I took out my wallet and counted out sixty dollars. I offered the notes to her. 'Sixty dollars.'

She sighed deeply her head bowed. 'You will have me go hungry?'

'I'm afraid so.'

My father who had not let on his understanding of

Spanish had to stifle his laughter with a cough. The woman looked up, a broad grin on her face. 'Sixty dollars,' she affirmed.

She shook my hand warmly and smiled happily at my father. She took the notes and counted them slowly and tucked them away between her breasts. She had still made a big profit. She rolled up the rug and thanked us again. Waving, she called after us from her shop doorway. 'If there is anything else you want please come back. You know I give a good deal. Goodnight, señores.'

The sale had paid the rent for a couple of weeks. We waved back, 'Buenas noches, señora.'

The next morning we flew back to Lima. I said goodbye to my father and told him I might be back in a year or so. He told me to stay away as long as I could. I thanked him for his concern.

Alone again in the hotel I looked forward to leaving Peru. It felt the most dangerous place I had been to. There was a violence simmering, and it looked ready to boil over.

I still had a day until my flight to Chile. I stayed in my hotel room. Political and social unrest was reported on the television and in the newspapers. That evening a young foreigner was shot dead in Lima. The Sendero Luminoso had raided a cheap boarding house, singled him out as a tourist and murdered him. I watched from my hotel room as a huge protest rally converged on San Martín Square.

The next morning there was a phone call from the travel agent. Could I go round to see them? The airline was the latest casualty of the unrest. They were all out on strike. I asked the tourist agent when the next flight was. They were all booked up; everyone was leaving the country. She couldn't get me a flight on another airline for three weeks. The airline on strike refused to refund my ticket.

The only other way out of the country was a four-day bus journey through the heart of bandit country. The tourist agent told me she would try her best to get me a refund. I went back to the hotel. There was a tank parked outside. The bus journey would be suicide.

I risked leaving my hotel to buy a packet of cigarettes. I was just walking back when two army assault vehicles screamed up the road. I ducked back into the hotel foyer as more army vehicles appeared from the back streets. Hundreds of people gathered in the square stampeded in all directions. Most were trapped. Within a minute the army had completely sealed San Martín Square. I watched as the police erected barricades around the mob and herded them with machine-guns into lorries. A few who had identity papers were allowed to leave. There was no explanation for the event in the papers the next day. I wanted to get the hell out of Peru.

I went round to the travel agent. The roads were unnaturally quiet and there was an obvious army presence. Now the only seat available for a month was a first class seat, in two days' time. I told her to book it. My father had paid for the original ticket with American Express. She said the airline company would accept the original ticket in part exchange for the first class ticket. I told her my father had now returned to England so he couldn't pay the difference. I was having to stay at the hotel paying forty dollars a night because the airline her company had recommended wouldn't fly me. She said that her company wouldn't pay the difference in air fare or my hotel bill. I told her I didn't have the money to pay the difference so she should put it on my father's bill.

After much conferring with the manager, they agreed to increase my father's bill. 'We are taking a great risk, señor. If your father does not agree to pay the difference, we will lose.'

'He will pay, don't worry.'

'You are sure? You have asked him?'

'Yes, no problem. I rang him this morning.' Desperate circumstances excuse desperate lies.

'We believe you to be honest. We will trust you.'

They gave me my first class ticket. I spent the evening in the hotel bar and caught a taxi to the airport first thing the next morning.

*

CHAPTER 26

First Class

I walked out to the plane and was escorted to my seat. I had bought the last-available first class ticket and there were only five other first class passengers. The stewardess took my denim jacket and hung it up with the Italian designer jackets of my fellow travellers. I was helped into my sofa-sized seat. The captain popped his head around the door and welcomed us to his plane. He shook hands and greeted by name the man sitting next to me.

When we were sitting comfortably the plane took off. On my seat was a bag of free gifts from the airline: a pack of cards, a pair of socks, postcards, envelopes, baggage labels and a rather dashing red and black blindfold.

We had two stewardesses to serve us. They brought out a newspaper trolley. I asked for an English paper. They handed me an American one. I said that I wanted a paper from England. They apologized profusely but this was the only English-language paper they had. I accepted it, shrugging, to emphasize that flying first class I expected a first class paper. I was appeased by another half bottle of champagne and a few smoked salmon appetizers. I skimmed through my newspaper until I found the cartoons, but they lost something in translation so I turned to chat to my neighbour. I noticed as he crossed his legs he was wearing silk socks. I'd never spoken to anyone who wore silk socks.

Rich South Americans are incredibly susceptible to Western culture. Just being English is usually recommendation enough for any introduction. Despite my denims, he presumed that, being English and travelling first class, I must be a gentleman of quality. Who was I to break his preconceptions? He exuded wealth and power. I decided to appeal to his snobbery. But how should I open the conversation?

'Pleasant champagne, tastes like a seventy-seven,' was a bit risky as I knew nothing of champagne. However, I did know about silk worms.

'I like your socks. Are they silk?'

'Yes, I bought them in Harrods.'

'Ah, really? I shop there often. [One Terry's Chocolate Orange back in seventy-five.] Have you been recently?'

'Not for a couple of years.'

'Do you speak English?'

He did and he had liked London very much, despite the hotel costing two hundred dollars a day. He waited for my response, clearly interested in my opinion of the price.

'Would that be considered expensive in South America?' I asked nonchalantly.

He was a cool customer and shrugged, saying, 'Somewhat.' He said he was interested because he had a string of hotels in Peru. I asked why he was going to Santiago. He told me he was a senator and was on his way to Buenos Aires with his football team. Combining football with politics was standard, though most South Americans believed football to be the more important of the two. This visit was to strengthen his personal ties with the Buenos Aires government. I discovered that his party was not in power so it was safe to ask about the disastrous shape of the Peruvian economy.

Peru is incredibly rich in natural resources. Peruvians have gas, oil, tin, silver and gold. They also have a great range of climates from tropical to mountainous desert. They should therefore be able to grow any sort of crop they require.

He explained to me that corruption was at the root of the problems. He said that government ministers preferred to import instead of using home products. The reason for this is that they receive large private commissions from the foreign multi-national companies for organizing the deals. He smiled at my horrified expression and said that the commission racket was in effect all around the world. It was just out of control in Peru.

He told the story of a Peruvian senator who went on a cultural exchange to the house of an American senator. The American had a beautiful home in the expensive suburbs of a city. The Peruvian was very impressed at the American's high standard of living. He commented that the American must be very independently wealthy to afford a house like this. The American smiled shrewdly and said, 'Not really.'

The Peruvian was baffled and so the American explained. He led the Peruvian to his front window and gestured down to the valley.

'Do you see that road and bridge down there?'

'*Sí.*'

'Well, I organized the building of that and ten per cent commission built this place.'

He patted his trouser pocket smugly. The Peruvian was very impressed.

A year later, the American went to Peru to complete the exchange. He drove up the three-mile, magnolia-lined drive of the Peruvian senator's home. He climbed the marble steps and was ushered in by a butler. He met the senator in the west wing of the palatial home. The American was very impressed. 'You must be very independently wealthy to own a home like this.'

The Peruvian smiled and took him to his twenty-foot plate-glass veranda.

'Do you see that road and bridge down there?'

'No.'

'Ah-ha, one hundred per cent commission built this place!'

All the first class passengers laughed as they had eavesdropped this story, which was clearly one of their favourites. He explained that the story was based on fact, but was the best-known Peruvian political joke.

In my naïveté I asked, 'How can politicians get away with the blatant corruption?' He answered that ninety-five per cent of the population were illiterate and most of the others accepted the corruption. They realized that, given the opportunity, they would do the same. What was needed in Peru was honest politicians. I said I thought that could apply for every country in the world. He said that he had already made his fortune and was just interested in doing his best for his country. He considered that he had a good chance of being the next Peruvian president.

'Do you have a daughter?' I inquired.

She was nineteen and at a finishing school in Switzerland. He gave me his address and said next time I was in Lima I must give him a ring. He smiled and said perhaps by then he might be in the Presidential Palace.

We broke for lunch, which was served from a silver trolley on silver plates. First course was crayfish, followed by a choice of local dishes, fish or a marinaded steak. My senator friend recommended the steak. I swilled it down with a bottle of imported French red wine. After caramel pudding and cheese and biscuits, I stretched out and fell to sleep. The five other first class passengers also snoozed in the luxurious space. Our pleasant stewardesses took the opportunity to polish the silver.

The stewardess woke me as we were about to land at Santiago. After touching down, I stood up and stretched. I took a peek behind the curtain at the economy class, who were out of their seats waiting to depart. They believed they were waiting for the doors to open and the steps to arrive. The steps, however, had arrived almost immediately and they were waiting for us (the first class passengers) to collect our jackets. While they waited patiently, my stewardess helped me into my denim jacket and wished me a pleasant trip.

We were a long way from the terminal so, while the other passengers were packed into stuffy airport buses, we were chauffeured to the check in. I said goodbye to the senator and walked straight through customs. My rucksack was waiting with the leather suitcases of the other first class passengers. I was out of the airport only minutes after leaving the plane. First class certainly had its advantages.

CHAPTER 27

CIAO

A modern airport coach drove us in air-conditioned luxury to the centre of Santiago. The wide roads were lined with expensive suburbs, the wealthy homes closeted by private hedges and ornate iron gates. Nearing the centre, the roads widened and the buildings grew. Of all the South American cities I had visited, Santiago was the most modern. The buildings of glass and concrete enclosed the few genuine plazas. However, the people were the most modern thing about the city. In many of the other large cities of South America the inhabitants are first-generation city dwellers. They have been drawn to the cities from their rural poverty by the usual bright-light dreams, such as running water, education and jobs. The people of Santiago were experienced city dwellers. They were fashionably dressed and they bustled about with stomach ulcer pace. Their feet seemed to stamp out a beat, 'Busy, busy, lots of work to do.'

The bus dropped me at the centre. There were several conferences being held in Santiago and so I'd only been able to get a room in a high class hotel. I couldn't afford to stay long at the price of thirty dollars a day, so I set about finding a plane. I asked at reception if they knew of a travel agent. The pretty young receptionist said she could ring around a few and find me the best price for a ticket to New Zealand. I left it with her, although I was sceptical of her helpfulness. She probably had a brother in the business.

I went to check out the scene. I needed to change some

money into the local currency, but all the official bureaus were closed for the day. There were no obvious street changers, so I presumed the black market was illegal. I knew, however, that if I walked around for long enough I would be approached. True enough, a voice said, '¿Cambio?'

A well-groomed young man leaning furtively against a pillar repeated, '¿Cambio?'

I nodded and he gestured for me to follow. I presumed we would walk a few yards off the street to make a deal. Instead he led me into a large building that housed many small businesses. He walked briskly past these offices, threatening to lose me in the crowd. I caught up as he descended an isolated staircase down into a dimly lit basement. I followed him into a particularly dim office and he gestured that I should sit down. The tout scurried off leaving me rather anxiously in this spurious underground bank.

Touts work on a commission basis, being paid a set fee for each client they bring in, irrespective of the size of deal.

A warty man looked up from his pot plant and eyed me stonily across a shabby wooden deak. '¿Cuánto?'

I only had hundred dollar bills and as I expected to stay a couple of days I decided to change seventy dollars. The boss took my hundred and leaned back in his chair. He shifted a picture on the wall behind him to reveal a square hole. A gnarled and bent pair of hands was visible counting notes through the secret hatch. He passed my bill through and let the picture swing back. We sat for a few seconds, his vacuous stare returning to the pot plant. Then there was a faint knock. He reopened the hatch and the crippled hand passed out some notes. I couldn't see a door and I imagined that it must be a deformed relative that had been given the job to save him from begging on the streets.

Other handicapped people that manage to survive childhood are often abandoned by families and, without a welfare state, they're left to grovel for pennies.

Still in my seat I counted the notes and checked for watermarks. I'd been warned that there were a lot of fake dollars on the market. I also wanted another chance to see behind the picture. No new business came into the shop so I left to look for a travel agent.

A travel agent tout escorted me to his shop and an incredible figure of one thousand four hundred dollars was quoted for the flight to New Zealand. Back at the hotel the receptionist had discovered a special offer of one thousand three hundred and sixty dollars that stopped at Easter Island and Tahiti. I just wanted to leave South America so I asked the address of the travel agent. She told me the agent would come to the hotel to save me the trouble.

Within half an hour the agent was in the foyer. She explained the stopovers and why the ticket was so expensive. All South American governments believe that if you can afford to fly out of their country, you should be able to pay the heavy departure taxes that account for over a third of the ticket price.

I couldn't get a flight for three days, but I decided to let her book provisionally. She assured me this would be done immediately. Leaving me with her card, she promised to contact me the next day.

Totally in tune with the ever-present corruption, I'd no intention of letting my money out of my sight until I'd checked her out. After an hour I rang the airport and discovered that they had just taken a reservation in my name. I had become so suspicious of South Americans, especially if they were extremely helpful, that I still wasn't satisfied. After all it was well within the realms of my experience that the woman had a colleague at the airport. After making the phone call I went to the address on her card. Much to my surprise, it was just an ordinary travel agent.

I returned to the hotel. I was sick of the paranoia. I wanted to relax, speak English. I was sick of South

America. I had hoped to spend my twenty-first birthday with my uncle in New Zealand, but now I would wait three days for departure.

The next day the travel agent returned with my tickets, and I gave her the cash. That day I was twenty-one and I was alone in a hotel in Santiago. I told the pretty receptionist that it was my birthday. She came out from behind the desk and gave me a big hug and kiss. Ever the optimist, I thought *Great, no need for a hot water bottle tonight!* But as my hand fell to her bottom, I realized why I was so fed up. It was not being alone on my birthday, it wasn't South America. I was missing Anita – her smile, her touch, her fiery temper.

Oh, no! It was a case of the dreaded and unspeakable begins with 'l' and rhymes with 'dove'.

I had previously thought a relationship was the length of time it took to meet carnally. No, perhaps this time I'd had a real relationship. One where I wanted to stay for lunch as well as breakfast. Maybe this meant I was now an adult. I hoped not. I considered myself far too young to talk at length about the weather. I had run away from all of that in England, but it had caught me up in the form of a woman, admittedly a beautiful form. It was painful to picture her in my mind. I would never see her again.

I tried to convince myself a few home-cooked meals in New Zealand would sort me out of this one-woman nonsense. I needed to get back in the swing of a totally superficial lifestyle. I had to put Anita out of my mind. *I will never see her again,* repeated in my head over and over again, censoring all thoughts, trying to barricade away all memories. I gave the receptionist's buttock a squeeze. It made no impression on my brooding melancholia.

I returned to my room and made a reverse charges telephone call to my family in England. I refused to hang up until I'd spoken to everyone. My sister told me not to rush back as she had redecorated my bedroom and moved in. Typically, my mother was worried about me. Perhaps

I should have written, but it had only been three months since my last postcard. She said she was happier now she knew which continent I was in. Wasn't the Southern Hemisphere enough? They wished me a happy twenty-first. I said I was having a wonderful time.

What was that? I almost felt a tear. *Catch a grip, you wimp!*

I lay back on my lonely double bed in my lonely hotel room, and wrote the first chapter of this book.

Early next morning, with solid determination I caught a taxi to the airport. Perhaps the anticipation of travelling again excited me or, more likely, my butterflies were suppressed panic. I felt I was desperately trying to walk slowly while thunderous black clouds closed in. All the immensely strong emotions South America had provoked were bearing down like some savage black bear. I longed to sit on the plane.

As I queued for check-in, a middle-aged woman tried to make conversation. I was fed up with the constant attention being a gringo brought. Everyone wanted to know your business. I pretended not to understand her Spanish. She didn't seem to care and she prattled on about her son and how she was on her way to visit him for the first time. She told me of the presents she had bought and his likes and dislikes. She nattered away for twenty minutes until we were almost at the front of the queue. She then started telling me that she had never been on an aeroplane before and she was very excited.

Throughout the last twenty minutes I hadn't said a word. She commented that she thought the baggage weight restrictions were very mean and she might not be able to take all the presents she had bought for her son.

She asked, as I only had one bag, if I might take one of hers. I shrugged pretending that I didn't understand. Turning away I lifted my bag on to the weighing scales and fumbled for my ticket. As the airline man took my ticket he gestured at the luggage, 'Is that your box?'

Confused, I looked down. The woman had put a box on the scales with my bag. I mumbled that it wasn't my box. He had seen the woman sneak it on to the scales.

'You can't take other people's luggage.'

The woman snatched it and disappeared into the crowd. Standing there, the horror of the situation struck home. There was no doubt in my mind that the box had been full of cocaine, the woman had vanished so quickly and suspiciously.

After all this time in South America I had been caught out, right at the last. If it hadn't been for the sharp eyes of the check-in man, two kilos of cocaine would have boarded that plane with my name tag stuck to it. It seemed as if I had just met my first honest South American official. I could have wept with gratitude.

I went through to the departure lounge and sat as far from everyone as possible. I didn't speak to anyone else in my last hour of South America.

It had drugged me, starved me, framed me, challenged me, excited me, loved me and I had survived, just. I did the fingers to it as I climbed aboard the plane, destination Easter Island, Tahiti and New Zealand. I was starting to realize that 'abroad' held no answers. Sooner or later, I'd have to return to England to face the future. But not quite yet. I still hadn't got a tan.

A Note to You

Amboro National Park is now financially secure and enlarged to 6,500 square kilometres. A new park called 'Huirkicocha' (Little Saucepan Lake) of similar size is proposed beside Amboro.

Guy is doing a national curassow survey for the world pheasant organization. Ornithologists are particularly interested in curassows because they are considered a conservation dipstick. They are a measure of conservation success as they tolerate no human interference. Through mapping their national distribution, it is hoped to identify areas for conservation priority.

Guy eventually found a horned curassow nest with one huge white egg. Since then the curassow has been left to its peaceful and secret seclusion.

My water lizards were 'preserved' and sent to Philadelphia University. They have still not been identified. I'm presently holding auditions for any young women who would like a lizard named after them. A certain propensity for child bearing is the main qualification.

Valerie is in London trying to raise funds for a film about conservation and how the money donated by the man in the street is spent.

Robin still works day and night to save the forest. He has done more for conservation than any man I know. I feel privileged to have been in a small way involved in his work.

Anita is well and, I hope, married.

I have changed my name, wear a false beard and am doing a European business degree in Turin, Italy.

Oliver Greenfield
January 1992

Index